Frege's Detour

John Perry is Emeritus Professor of Philosophy at Stanford University and at the University of California, Riverside. He received his BA from Doane College in 1964 and his PhD from Cornell University in 1968. Perry was the founder- and for many years the co-host-of the nationally syndicated radio show *Philosophy Talk*. He is also the co-author of the market leading *Introduction to Philosophy*, now in its ninth edition. Perry taught at UCLA from 1968 to 1974, before joining Stanford University. He worked at Stanford until his retirement in 2008, and subsequently taught part time at the University of California, Riverside until 2013.

T0352071

CONTEXT AND CONTENT

SERIES EDITOR: François Recanati, Institut Nicod

Frege's Detour

An Essay on Meaning, Reference, and Truth

JOHN PERRY

Philosophy Departments
Stanford University
University of California, Riverside

OXFORD
UNIVERSITY PRESS

OXFORD
UNIVERSITY PRESS

Great Clarendon Street, Oxford, OX2 6DP,
United Kingdom

Oxford University Press is a department of the University of Oxford.
It furthers the University's objective of excellence in research, scholarship,
and education by publishing worldwide. Oxford is a registered trade mark of
Oxford University Press in the UK and in certain other countries

First published 2019

First published in paperback 2021

Published in the United States of America by Oxford University Press
198 Madison Avenue, New York, NY 10016, United States of America

British Library Cataloguing in Publication Data
Data available

Library of Congress Cataloging in Publication Data
Data available

ISBN 978-0-19-881282-1 (Hbk.)
ISBN 978-0-19-285964-8 (Pbk.)

To the memory of
Jon Barwise
Hector-Neri Castañeda
Gareth Evans
Montgomery Furth
David Lewis
Fellow admirers of Frege, who left us too soon.

Preface

The thinking for this book began in 1975. I was trying to write a book on personal identity during my sabbatical. I did not finish the book, and still have not. I spent my sabbatical stuck on the problem of self-knowledge. At first I was pretty confident I could deal with it. On my desk was a mimeographed draft of what eventually became David Kaplan's "On the Logic of Demonstratives." I was sure that what I needed to understand about the logic and semantics of "I" was contained therein. Also on the desk was a copy of Shoemaker's *Self-Knowledge and Self-Identity* (1963) plus more some of his more recent work, in particular "Self-Reference and Self-Awareness" (1968). I had studied with Shoemaker at Cornell. Virtually everything Shoemaker said seemed right to me, but I thought it needed to be connected more firmly with issues in the philosophy of language. And there was a copy of Geach and Black's *Translations From the Philosophical Writings of Gottlob Frege*. Although I went to Cornell with the intention of studying Wittgenstein, in the end I wrote my dissertation on Frege, Geach, and identity. There was a sheaf of articles and chapters from Hector-Neri Castañeda, whose important ideas Harry Deutsch had brought to my attention and explained to me.

I had no doubt that many philosophers understood each of the philosophers on my desk much better than I did. But I suspected that very few understood all of them all as well as I did. And I was sure that their works, taken together, provided what was needed to for an account self-knowledge and its expression in language. It was just up to me to dig it out. But I could not. Frege's theory of sense and reference seemed right. Kaplan's theory of indexicals seemed right. Castañeda's insights and his wonderful examples had to be dealt with. Shoemaker's concept of criteria of identity and first-person immunity to error through misidentification had to find a place in my more semantical approach. But they just did not fit together. I had set a side couple of months to write the self-knowledge chapter. By the end of that time, I was more confused than ever.

I never finished the chapter, much less the rest of the book. But at one point, pretty late in the sabbatical, I had what felt like a revelation. Perhaps Frege was not quite right about cognitive significance. Perhaps Kaplan's "characters" could provide what was missing in his account, even though they seemed to present a problem. By the end of the sabbatical I had come up with a long paper explaining what I felt I had come to understand about the problem. On the advice of Julius Moravcsik, I split it to two shorter articles, published as "Frege on Demonstratives" (Perry, 1977) and "The Problem of the Essential Indexical" (Perry, 1979).

Since then I have been on my own long detour. Personal identity and self-knowledge have pretty much had to wait, until I digest all the insights gathered on my desk 43 years ago, or at least come closer than I did then. This has led to work with Jon Barwise on situation semantics, where we tried to generalize Kaplan's insights into a relational theory of meaning; breathe some new life into situations, circumstances, and states of affairs, pretty much pushed off stage by Frege and Church; take account of what Michael Turvey taught us about ecological psychology; and, unshackled by the extensionalist tendencies we saw in Davidson, develop what he called for, an innocent account of the attitudes. It led to work with David Israel, where we developed the concepts of reflexive, referential, and incremental content, and with him and Syun Tutiya on information and action. It led to Mark Crimmins explaining to me why I needed episodes in my account, and how the concept of unarticulated constituents could be helpful in understanding attitude reports, and what went wrong with the account in the book I wrote with Barwise, *Situations and Attitudes*. It led to a lot of work with Kepa Korta and others on how pragmatics can put the reflexive/referential distinction to good use.

It was traumatic, in 1975, to come to the conclusion that Frege was wrong about something. I had written a dissertation that defended Frege on identity against Peter Geach, a brilliant philosopher whose work I greatly admired. It was hard for me to accept that he did not have cognitive significance quite right.

Since then, a number of eminent philosophers have argued that I was wrong about Frege in "Frege on Demonstratives," but I still think I was basically right. A couple of years ago, I returned to working pretty seriously on Frege. For the first time I studied his *Begriffsschrift* in some detail. This led to the current book, which probably will not convince the eminent critics who still live, and would not convince Gareth Evans or Michael Dummett were they still alive and motivated to read it. I am still on my detour. But I hope to get straight about personal identity before I die. If, contrary to my expectation, there is an afterlife, I do not want to have an identity crisis when I get there.

Many people have helped me with this book, especially the members of a weekly seminar held via Zoom: Kepa Korta, Maria Ponte, Richard Vallee, Chris Genovesi, Eros Corazza, Armando Lavalle, Kenneth Olson, Genoveva Marti and on occasion Dan Flickinger, Prashant Parikh, Carl Hoefer, and Darren Bradley, and Jenny Hung who discussed the ideas with me, and some of whom have commented on many many drafts. I am indebted to my colleagues at Stanford and UC Riverside, and many students, graduate and undergraduate, who have shared many ideas and helped me keep my thinking straight over the years. Among graduate students, I am especially indebted to Mark Crimmins, now a colleague, Lisa Hall, who explained to me what folk psychology was all about (Hall, 1993), and Leora Weitzman, whose dissertation on individuating contents and Frege's idea of carving up content taught me a lot (Weitzman, 1989).

In the course of writing the book I have been fortunate to have many conversations with the brilliant computer scientist Carl Hewett, particularly about higher-order logic. He has explained a lot of things to me, some of which I managed to understand. He thinks the important detour relevant to Frege is the one logic took away from Frege's path, which leads to higher order logic, veering off instead towards first-order logic and set theory. See (Hewitt, 2015). We were often joined by Dan Flickinger; a great proportion of the little I understand about modern linguistics is due to Flickinger.

I have learned a lot about Frege from Edward Zalta, both in conversation and from his articles. Zalta has used his impressive theory of abstract objects to interpret Frege's Thoughts; his may be the best account we have that is based on a thoroughly worked out axiomatic theory (Zalta, 1983, 1988).

There are many, many others who deserve mention, but if I try to mention all, I will leave out some. My wife Frenchie, my three children and my ten grandchildren have all been very supportive as I spend hours on this book that could have been spent on other things that would have been more fun for them, and no doubt for me too. Finally, over the past dozen years or so, Ken Taylor has been a constant source of good conversation and deep ideas, as we co-hosted the radio program "Philosophy Talk." Ken was very understanding when, in the throes of trying to finish this book, I had to leave the program, and I'm grateful to Deborah Satz and Josh Landy for taking over my duties. Go to the KALW website (KALW.org) and catch the program.

This book grew out of lectures I gave in Paris at the invitation of François Recanati. I owe a great debt to Recanati, for his ideas, for his sympathetic treatment of my ideas, and many more practical favors he has extended to me over many years. Peter Momtchiloff at Oxford University Press has been helpful and encouraging and, last but not least, two anonymous referees for the Press provided helpful and insightful comments.

October 2018 John Perry

Contents

1

Introduction

> Identity gives rise to challenging questions which are not alto-
> gether easy to answer. Is it a relation? A relation between objects,
> or between names or signs of objects? In my *Begriffsschrift* I
> assumed the latter.
>
> (Gottlob Frege, "On Sense and Denotation")[1]

Thus begins Gottlob Frege's 1892 a Essay, "Über Sinn und Bedeutung",
"On Sense and Denotation."[2] No essay was more influential in analytic
philosophy of language in the twentieth century. It was, and still is,
required reading in virtually every analytically oriented philosophy of
language class. The questions Frege asks about meaning, reference, and
truth remain central concerns of the philosophy of language. Those
who provide different answers to these questions commonly take Frege's
answers as their starting point, as I shall in this book. As indebted
as philosophy and logic are to Frege, however, I think this essay put
philosophy on a detour. The aim of this book is exploring how we can
appreciate Frege's insights, but avoid the detour.

1.1 The Detour

Frege begins "On Sense and Denotation" by returning to problems
with identity that he first encountered in his earlier work, the 1879

---

[1] As translated by Max Black, (Frege, 1960a).
[2] Black uses "reference" as a translation for "*Bedeutung*." I have changed this to "denotation"
for reasons explained below.

Frege's Detour: An Essay on Meaning, Reference, and Truth. John Perry, Oxford University Press (2019).
© John Perry DOI: 10.1093/oso/9780198812821.001.0001

Begriffsschrift, and criticizing the treatment of the problems he gave there. The book *Begriffsschrift* is named for the language he develops in it, which (following J. L Austin in his translation of Frege's *Grundlagen* (Frege, 1950)) I will call "Concept-Writing." In the *Begriffsschrift* Frege's invented quantification theory and first and second order logic.

In the *Begriffsschrift*, Frege uses the term "circumstance" (*Umstand*) for what sentences refer to (*bedeuten*). It seems that this is the term he found intuitive for what he had in mind. He does not treat it as a technical term, or give us any special explanation. It is natural to take circumstances to be structures made up of objects, properties, and relations. If the objects have the properties, or stand in the relations, we have *facts* or *truths*. Frege uses "falling under" for this structure. Objects *fall under* properties and relations.

But Frege also sees the falling-under structure at higher levels, where properties and relations fall under appropriate properties and relations. I will call these higher level possibilities "property-structures." Property-structures are the key to many of Frege's enduring contributions. We should not see "Caesar exists" as saying that Caesar falls under the property of existence. It rather tells us that the property of being identical with Caesar falls under the property of being instantiated; there is someone who is Caesar. "Birds have feathers" does not tell us that some object named "birds" is feathered; it tells us that a relation holds between the property of being a bird and the property of having feathers; objects that have the first property have the second.

Taking circumstances to be the contents of sentences about objects seemed to give rise to problems with identity sentences. Frege proposed a solution in the *Begriffsschrift*. In the opening of "On Sense and Denotation" he rejects that solution, before explaining his new theory of sense and denotation; circumstances have no role in this theory. What was the problem with them?

If we read "=" as identity, as Frege does and I will do, then, if "A = B" is true, then "A = A" and "A = B" stand for the same circumstance. The same object is denoted twice in each sentence, and the relation predicated is the same, identity. But somehow we can learn something from the second sentence that we cannot learn from the first, that the two names co-denote. On Frege's conception of logic and content, sentences with the same content should support the same inferences. From "A = B" and "$\phi(A)$" we can infer "$\phi(B)$". But we cannot infer this from "A = A". Something has gone wrong.

In the *Begriffsschrift* Frege's solution is to provide us with a new sign, "≡" for the relation he calls *identity of content* which holds between names when their contents, that is the objects they refer to, are identical. The new sign:

> ... expresses the circumstance that two names have the same content ((Frege, 1967), Section 20).

Frege uses "=" twice in the *Begriffsschrift*, in Section 1 and Section 5, before he introduces "≡". He reinstates "=" after the *Begriffsschrift*. But there, his solution to his identity problems is to retire "=" in favor of "≡."

In "On Sense and Denotation," after criticizing his *Begriffsschrift* account, Frege introduces his new theory:

> It is natural, now, to think of there being connected with a sign (name, combination of words, letter), besides that to which the sign denotes, which may be called the denotation of the sign, also what I would like to call the sense of the sign, wherein the mode of presentation is contained ((Frege, 1960a), p. 59).

On this theory the "information-value" of a sentence (at a first pass, whether it is analytic or synthetic) and its "cognitive value" (basically, the belief a sincere and semantically competent speaker expresses with it) depend on the senses of the names it contains, not their denotations.[3] The sense of the sentence as a whole Frege calls a "Thought." Sentences *express* Thoughts. So "A = A" and "A = B" express different Thoughts, and the problem is solved, or so it seems. The sense of an expression seems to be basically the properties an object must have, and the relations it must have to other things, to be the denotation of the expression, according to the definitions and other conventions and practices of the language. In the case of "perfect" languages, as Concept-Writing was intended

---

[3] While Frege sometimes seems to equate the issue of whether a sentence is informative or not with whether it is synthetic or analytic, Horty shows the issue is more complicated, for both interpretive and philosophical reasons (Horty, 2007).

to be, speakers should assign the same senses to expressions. In the case of "imperfect" languages, a category to which all natural languages belong, the senses associated with expressions may differ from speaker to speaker. So Thoughts do not involve objects, as circumstances do, but rather the senses associated with the names that denote the objects. This basic characterization is not an exhaustive account of how Frege thought of his senses, but I think it is the core; it fits all of the examples and explanations that Frege provides in "On Sense and Denotation" and other essays and writings from the same period—what I will call the "1890 Essays."[4]

Frege emphasizes that Thoughts are not episodes of thinking, but abstract objects that are "grasped" in thinking, that provide the contents or truth-conditions of such episodes, and the sentences we use to express them.[5] One might expect circumstances to be the denotations of sentences. But Frege instead maintains that that we are "driven" to accept truth-values as the denotations of sentences. All of this takes up no more than a third of the essay.

Then the bulk of the essay is spent defending this last doctrine, that sentences denote truth-values, from an objection. On Frege's principles, the denotation of an expression with significant parts must be a function of the denotations of those parts. This means that substitution of co-denoting expressions in a larger expression preserves the denotation of the larger expression. But then the doctrine that sentences denote truth-values seems to have many counter-examples. The sentences "Berkeley is west of Santa Cruz" and "Mogadishu is the capital of Somalia" are both true. But not everyone who believes that Berkeley is west of Santa Cruz believes that Mogadishu is the capital of Somalia, and vice-versa. If Smith is a person of the first sort, then the first report below is true while the second is false.

---

[4] After the *Begriffsschrift*, Frege's next book was *The Foundations of Arithmetic* (Frege, 1884). He developed a key idea for his magnum opus, *Grundgesetze*, (Frege, 1893/1903) that numbers are the extensions of concepts ((Frege, 1950), Section 68). Then, before writing the *Grundgesetze* he developed his theory of sense and denotation in a series of essays written in the early 1890s, "Function And Concept," "Concept and Object," and "On Sense and Denotation"(Frege, 1960a). These, together with an important letter to Husserl and an unpublished manuscript from the same period comprise what I call the "1890 Essays."[Frege, 1967a, 1967b, 1960a, 1891b, 1891b, 1891c.] The theory becomes more nuanced when he returns to the issue of sense after the *Grundgesetze*.

[5] I capitalize "Thought" when using it for Frege's Thoughts.

(1)   Smith believes that Berkeley is west of Santa Cruz

(2)   Smith believes that Mogidishu is the capital of Somalia

But (2) results from (1) by substitution of one true sentence for another. We could generate the same problem for

(3)   Smith says that Berkeley is west of Santa Cruz.

Something has gone wrong. Frege's Detour begins with his solution.

His solution is the doctrine of *indirect denotation*. Sentences do not always denote truth-values. Sometimes they denote themselves, as when they are enclosed in quotation marks. And, Frege says, they sometimes denote their ordinary senses, the Thoughts they ordinarily express. This is what happens in indirect discourse and attitude reports. In (1), (2), and (3). the embedded sentences denote their usual senses, Thoughts which are not the same. So the substitution is not permitted. Problem solved. Or so it seems.

I do not think the doctrine of indirect denotation solved any problems; it created many, however. The doctrine reinforces and reflects a number of views about truth and cognition which are wrong:

(A)   The content of a sentence, basically its truth-conditions, can be captured by a unique proposition;

(B)   This proposition is the *cognitive significance* of the sentence for semantically competent speakers and hearers, in particular:
   (i)   This proposition is *what is said* by someone who uses the sentence
   (ii)   This proposition is *what is believed* by a sincere and semantically competent speaker;

(C)   Such propositions are the denotations or referents of that-clauses in indirect discourse and attitude reports;

(D)   Beliefs (and other attitudes) are relations to propositions.

This detour starts with the challenging questions posed by identity. Already, Frege's conception of what logic is all about committed him to something akin to (A) and (B). But he eventually realized this simply does not square with circumstances as conceptual contents. If "A = B" is true, it refers to the same circumstance as does "A = A". But the two sentences do not have the same cognitive value; one could sincerely deny the first while sincerely asserting the second. Frege came to think of his *Begriffsschrift* solution as unsatisfactory, and abandoned the theory of conceptual content in favor of the theory of sense and denotation.

I will argue that circumstances and the theory of conceptual content provide something needed for semantics not provided by the theory of sense and denotation. Circumstances should not have been thrown out of the theory. The theory of sense and reference contains some important additional insights, but they can be incorporated into the theory of conceptual content. So, at least according to me, what Frege should have done is abandon (A) and all of its consequences. Without (A), and with a little common sense, his *Begriffsschrift* theory can deal with all of the challenges identity gives rise to, incorporate the insights of the theory of sense and denotation, and keep us off the detour. And, with a little more common sense, we can adapt the theory to an episode based account, that does not take the attitudes to consist of relations to propositions, and abandon (D).

1.2 Disclaimer

This book includes a fair amount of Frege interpretation. But, even on topics central to the argument, the interpretation is not comprehensive. This is most clear in my interpretation of Frege's Thoughts. Frege developed the concept between the *Begriffsschrift* and his 1980 Essays. I think the interpretation I offer helps us understand the functions of Thoughts, and to evaluate his arguments for indirect reference. But Frege faced problems with Thoughts that, as far as I can see, he couldn't resolve. Frege says that in the denotation of a sentence, all that is specific is lost. "Lincoln was a Republican" and "The sea is salty" are about different things having different properties, but they both denote the True. But all that is specific is not lost in Thoughts. The two sentences express quite different Thoughts; that is the job of of Thoughts, to capture subtle differences in truth-conditions, and thus provide an account of cognitive significance.

But the demands of Frege's analysis of number and arithmetic seems to require that Thought not be individuated completely in terms of the entities they are intuitively about. Consider this example, based on the *Grundlagen*, from Leora Weitzman ((Weitzman, 1989) p. 16).

The direction of Seventh Street is the same as the direction of Ocean Avenue.

Seventh Street is parallel to Ocean Avenue.

In Frege's metaphor, the two sentences carve up the same content in different ways. The first involves two directions and identity, the second two streets and being parallel. The idea that the same content can be carved up in different ways is present in the *Begriffsschrift*, as we shall see. It is crucial to the strategy Frege developed in the *Grundlagen* for his treatment of number. But it is puzzling and somewhat problematic for Thoughts, given one of their jobs, to account for differences in cognitive significance. It seems that, even setting objects aside, as not involved in Thoughts, a difference in the properties and relations denoted by different sentences will almost always produce some possibility that a reasonably competent speaker could believe one and at least have momentary doubts about the other. This is all related to the issues Horty discusses in *Frege on Definitions* (2007).

Weitzman argues quite persuasively that there is no single solution to the problem of individuating Thoughts that satisfies all the various criteria Frege suggests and that the various proposals for the nature of propositions on offer in contemporary philosophy are responsive to various strands in Frege's thinking. At one extreme, if we think of propositions as sets of possible worlds, subject matter seems to be lost. There is only one necessary proposition, no matter whether the necessary truth is a matter of properties considered by arithmetic, or geometry, or chemistry or anything else.[6] There are many proposals toward the other end of the spectrum, none which does everything Frege would have wanted.

---

[6] See (Perry, 1989).

Frege demanded a lot from the contents of sentences. He expected his Thoughts to provide truth-conditions for sentences, and also their cognitive significance. When one adds to this pair of duties the idea of carving up content, which seems to imply that propositions have no ultimate structure, one has given content a triad of duties that are difficult to reconcile. As Weitzman concludes, "Frege provides no criterion that is both noncircular and compatible with a proposition's having more than one ultimate structure."((Weitzman, 1989) p. iv).

I do not attempt to provide such a criterion. I try to provide an account of Thoughts that fits with what I take to be those of Frege's insights most relevant to the philosophy of language, and show that they do not lead to the Detour. Eventually, I will argue that the doctrine of unique content led Frege and many other philosophers ask too much of Thoughts and propositions. Contemporary philosophy provides a plethora of abstract objects as candidates for capturing the truth-conditions of sentences. This is not such a bad thing, if we give up the idea that there has to be one winning candidate.

1.3 The Plan

In Chapters 2 and 3 I discuss the *Begriffsschrift*. In Chapter 2 I focus on the theory of conceptual content that supported the wonderful innovations of that work. In Chapter 3 I discuss the problems that various examples involving identity posed for his account, and the conclusion that Frege eventually drew, that led to his replacing the theory of conceptual content with his theory of sense and denotation.

In Chapter 4 I discuss Frege's theory of sense and denotation as presented in the 1890 Essays, and in Chapter 5 as presented in the most famous of them, "On Sense and Denotation," where the argument for indirect denotation occurs.

After the *Begriffsschrift* Frege wrote *The Foundations of Arithmetic*, where he developed key ideas in his project of reducing arithmetic to logic. He develops an account of concepts and extensions, which played a key role in his strategy. Frege's extensions are not the extensions of modern set theory, but functions related to them.

In the 1890 Essays Frege develops his theory of sense and denotation, and he builds his theory of concepts and extension into the new theory. However, he does not discuss these developments in "On Sense and Denotation," which considers the sense and denotation of names and sentences, but not of concept words. (Frege uses "names" for both ordinary names, simple nouns that denote objects, and for definite descriptions. So his category of names basically coincides with what we now call "singular terms.") He refers readers elsewhere if they are interested in his treatment of concept-words. Thus, in his most famous and influential essay, at least for philosophers of language, we get only a part of his theory. It is this partial theory, combined with a simple treatment of concept words suggested by what he says about names, that has proven so influential in that field. And it is in terms of the partial theory that he justifies the doctrine of indirect denotation. My strategy is to explain, as best I can, the treatment of concept words we find other 1890 Essays, but to (mostly) bracket these complications in discussing "On Sense and Denotation," where they play no (explicit) role.

In Chapter 6 I provide my own solution to Frege's problems with identity and circumstances, within what I call the "reflexive-referential" theory. This solution was available to Frege within the *Begriffsschrift* theory, had he not been wedded to the doctrine of unique content. On my account neither "=" or circumstances are the problem, the problem is the doctrine of unique content.

In Chapter 7 I say more about circumstances. I argue that the argument in "On Sense and Denotation" for the conclusion that truth-values should be the denotations of sentences have no force against circumstances as a candidate for that role. I also consider Alonzo Church's argument in favor of truth-values, now usually called "the slingshot."

In Chapter 8 I develop a variant to Frege's theory of sense and reference, based on replacing truth-values with circumstances as the denotations of sentences. The theory of the *Begriffsschrift* is integrated with the theory of sense and denotation. I argue that while Thoughts are suitable for encoding the truth-conditions of sentences, circumstances are suitable for capturing what I call the "information significance" of sentences, which we must do to understand imperfect languages. I develop an innocent theory of attitude reports and direct discourse within this account, adopting a pragmatic account of "opacity," in the spirit of much work in the philosophy of language since the 1970s. But this account still basically treats the attitudes as relations to propositions. In Chapter 9 I argue that we need to take a further step to have a suitable framework for understanding the attitudes and indirect discourse. We need to bring episodes—thoughts and utterances—directly into the theory. I argue that to understand how the causal roles and contents of such episodes fit together, we need to understand what I call the reflexive and hybrid truth-conditions of these episodes. Once we have done that, I argue, we can deal with certain cases of opacity which the pragmatic strategy by itself cannot handle. I end the chapter, and the book, by adapting the account to deal with "today," "tomorrow," and other indexicals. I argue that we need to see Frege's senses as a special case of what I call "roles," which are my version of Kaplan's characters, to understand the causal roles of beliefs that we use indexicals to express.

1.4 Terminology

The translation of Frege's important term "*Bedeutung*" has been a matter of some controversy, helpfully explained by Michael Beaney in the introduction to his excellent collection of Frege translations (Beaney, 1997). Russell, in his appendix on Frege in *The Principles of Mathematics*, translates "*Sinn*" as "meaning" and "*Bedeutung*" as "indication" (Russell, 1903: p. 510). Later, in "On Denoting," he uses "meaning" and "denotation." Max Black and Peter Geach, in the original edition of their influential translations (1952), used "sense" for "Sinn" and "reference" for "*Bedeutung*." In later editions, they used "meaning" for "'Bedeutung.'" In the first English translation of "*Über Sinn und Bedeutung*"(Frege, 1949). Herbert Feigl used "nominatum" for "*Bedeutung*." Edward Zalta, in his important articles on Frege in the *Stanford Encyclopedia of Philosophy*, translates "*Bedeutung*" as "denotation."

I use "reference" as a translation for "'*Bedeutung*'" when it occurs in the *Begriffsschrift*, its original home. I use "denotation" when it occurs in the theory of *Sinn und Bedeutung*.[7] I use "reference" in more or less its standard use in contemporary philosophy of language when explaining my own view. These choices are not based on any particular insights about translation. Frege's concept of *Bedeutung* changes in important ways when he moves from conceptual content to the theory of sense and denotation, as he himself emphasized. It is useful to have two terms to mark the difference. My practice may suggest that Frege uses different German terms; I hereby cancel that suggestion.

Linguistically, "meaning" is probably the most straightforward translation of "*Bedeutung*," especially in the *Begriffsschrift*, where the distinction between sense and denotation has not been made. It is the translation Austin uses in *The Foundations of Arithmetic*, his translation of *Die Grundlagen der Arithmetik* (Frege, 1950). But, confusingly, it has also been used as a translation for "*Sinn*." Tyler Burge has documented how misleading the term can be in translating Frege (Burge, 1979). I do not use it as a translation of either term.

The term "reference" has become ubiquitous in the philosophy of language, due in part to Frege's huge influence and its use as a translation for *Bedeutung* in the original Max Black translation of "*Über Sinn und Bedeutung*." The use of the term in contemporary philosophy of language is heavily influenced by discussions of issues that emerged in the 1970s, when philosophers began to struggle to leave the Detour, a philosophical movement Howard Wettstein has called "The New Theory of Reference" (Wettstein, 1986). Criticisms and defenses of Frege's views were central to this movement, At least in the beginning, especially in Kripke's seminal work (Kripke, 1980). "reference" was used as a translation for "*Bedeutung*," and then became the standard term for discussion of the relation names have to the things they name, independently of Frege's views.[8]

I will say a bit more about how I use the expression "cognitive significance." Frege sometimes uses the term "information value" for a difference between "A = B" and "A = A", that the first is synthetic

---

[7] I make these substitutions in translations, which are otherwise left intact unless noted.

[8] Feigl's "nominatum" for "*Bedeutung*" has the virtue of emphasizing the close connection between naming and *Bedeutungen* in Frege's thinking, but it did not catch on. Zalta's use of "denotation" in his article on the *Grundgesetze* in the *Stanford Encyclopedia of Philosophy* gives me confidence it is a good choice for Frege's theory from 1890 on.

and the second analytic. In "Function and Concept" he recognizes that the problems identity poses are not confined to identity sentences and differences in information-value in this sense:

> If we say "The Evening Star is a planet with a shorter period of revolution than the Earth", the thought we express is other than in the sentence "The Morning Star is a planet with a shorter period of revolution than the Earth"; for somebody who does not know that the Morning Star is the Evening Star might regard one as true and the other as false ((Frege, 1960a), p. 138).

I use "cognitive significance" for the difference in such cases. Frege sometimes uses "cognitive value." Frege takes the cognitive value to be the Thought expressed by a sentence, or the relevant part of it. I offer a somewhat different account, so it is sometimes useful to have a similar but different term.

The cognitive significance of an utterance is what a sincere and semantically competent speaker must believe to make the utterance, and what a semantically competent and credulous hearer can learn from the utterance.

It might be better to use the phrase "semantic cognitive significance," although I will not. Consider this example. We are having dinner, and you say, "My steak needs salt." If you are sincere and semantically competent, you will believe that your steak needs salt. And if I trust you and am semantically competent, I will learn that your steak needs salt.

If I am not only semantically competent, but have rudimentary social skills, I will also learn that you would like me to pass you the salt. And you probably believed that saying "My steak needs salt" was likely to induce me to have such a belief, and pass you the salt. But those beliefs are not part of the semantic cognitive significance, or, as I shall use the term in this book, the "cognitive significance." They are not part of the truth-conditions of your remark. They are beliefs that a socially apt person will infer from other beliefs gained in virtue of semantic competence.

2
Frege's *Begriffsschrift*: Accomplishments

> Though small in size, [the *Begriffsschrift*] is perhaps Frege's
> greatest and most enduring achievement.... In fact many of his
> innovations in logic are so solidly incorporated into the body
> of contemporary logic that it has become difficult to appreciate
> Frege's originality in conceiving them.
>
> ((Hans Sluga, 1980), p. 65)

In the *Begriffsschrift* Frege developed the logical language he stayed with
throughout his career, Concept-Writing. Frege's revolutionary ideas, and
in particular his theory of quantification, played a huge role in the development of modern logic, and have been incorporated into the predicate
calculus we learn in introductory logic. As Sluga observes, that makes it
easy to overlook the genius involved in coming up with these ideas, which
solved problems that had puzzled many generations of brilliant logicians
and philosophers.

   In this chapter I first remind the reader of some important innovations
of the *Begriffsschrift*. Then I explain the semantic framework he used,
which he called "conceptual content," and say a bit about circumstances
which seem to play an important role in this intuitive framework, and led
to Frege's problems with identity.

2.1 Frege's Innovations

Concept-Writing includes many ideas that were incorporated into the
language of modern logic. One idea which did not take hold was Frege's
two-dimensional notation. Peano's linear notation won out over Frege's
two-dimensional script. I think Frege's notation is quite wonderful, and
I will use it a bit in this chapter to give the reader a taste of it. It seems

Frege's Detour: An Essay on Meaning, Reference, and Truth. John Perry, Oxford University Press (2019).
© John Perry DOI: 10.1093/oso/9780198812821.001.0001

that Frege was out of touch with his logical colleagues when he said, "the comfort of the typewriter is certainly not the *summum bonum*" ((van Heijenoort, 2002), 2). But perhaps he was simply ahead of his time. The notation is available in Latex, with the usepackage "frege." Is it one more of Frege's great ideas, which twenty-first century technology will help us appreciate?[1]

A basic idea that did catch on was his treatment of predicates as analogous to functions in mathematics. We learn early on in logic courses to think of an expression such as "$F(a)$" as an atomic sentence, made up of the predicate symbol "F" and a name "a", which is true if the object named by "a" meets the condition corresponding to "F". "$R(b, c)$" says the objects named by "b" and "c" stand in the relation corresponding to "R". The predicates in the predicate calculus come with empty places, or with variables indicating argument places. So we see that "$F()$" and "$F(x)$" provide properties, or unary conditions, or one-place relations, whereas "$R(,)$" or "$R(x, y)$" show us that we are dealing with a binary relation. We are taught to use "x" and "y" and "z" as variables, and "a" and "b" and "c", as names.

Those lucky enough to have been taught some grammar in elementary school will know that "Caesar conquers Gaul" is traditionally seen as made up of a subject term, "Caesar" and a predicate, "conquers Gaul." The predicate is the whole verb phrase. But when we take a logic course and are asked to symbolize the sentence, we will ignore that; this is what Frege taught us to do; he thought the subject-predicate structure found in natural language is misleading as to logical structure. The subject-predicate structure does not occur in Concept-Writing. The correct symbolization is "*Conquers(Caesar, Gaul)*." Gaul does not get lost in the "predicate" but has equal status with Caesar, one of two objects that stand in the relation of the first conquering the second, if the sentence is true.

Thus "*Conquers(x, y)*", what is now called a "predicate" in logic, is a sort of incomplete sentence; the "x" and "y" show where we need to insert names to have a complete one. Borrowing again from mathematics, Frege saw the names "Caesar" and "Gaul" as providing *arguments*, just as "2" and "4" provide arguments when we go from "$x + y$" to "$2 + 4$." The latter

---

[1] Probably not. Even those of us who admire Frege's notation, do not use it except to discuss Frege.

expression is what Frege calls a "name", a name for the number 6. The first expression is incomplete; it does not name anything, until arguments are supplied for "x" and "y".

In the *Begriffsschrift* Frege called properties "concepts" and one-place predicates "concept-words." He usually does not call relations "concepts," but simply "relations." Frege wrote at a time when logic was coming to grip with relations.[2] He explains binary relations in terms of functions, and does not simply conflate the categories of properties and relations.

We now tend to think in terms of a general category that includes properties and relations. Properties are a subcategory of relations, unary relations. But, somewhat oddly, it is natural to use "properties" for the category, no doubt for historical reasons. I will follow this somewhat convoluted practice. When I say "properties" I will almost always mean "properties and relations" and I will make the exceptions clear. When using Frege's term, "concept" I mean to include relations, unless specifically noted.

In the *Begriffsschrift*, Frege regards concept-words and relation-words as functional expressions. In later works, he explicitly regards both concepts and relations themselves as functions. I think this idea is implicit in the *Begriffsschrift*, and seeing it there helps make sense of things, but this is controversial. In my view he somewhat inchoately sees concepts as functions from arguments to circumstances in the *Begriffsschrift* and then quite explicitly as functions from arguments to truth-values in the theory of sense and denotation.

The German is "*Begriff*," and the name of his language derives from the central role he saw concepts as playing in logic. Concepts are not mental structures but objective properties and relations. "Concept" is the most natural term to use with Frege's important phrase "falling under." So I will use both "predicate" and "concept-word" depending on context, and similarly with "property" and "concept."

According to Frege's way of looking at things, complete expressions, including sentences, are importantly analogous to names. When we complete "$x + y$" with "2" and "4" we get a name of "six". When we complete "x conquered y" with "Caesar" and "Gaul," we also basically get a name. But of what? Frege's change of mind on this issue is a major difference

---

[2] See (Olson, 1987).

between the *Begriffsschrift* and his later theory of sense and denotation. In the *Begriffsschrift* he took sentences to refer to circumstances; in his later theory, he took them to denote truth-values. The whole idea that sentences stand for things analogous to the way that names do is explicit and argued for in "On Sense and Denotation." In the *Begriffsschrift* we have to look for it, but I think it is there to be found. Frege is not too scrupulous about use and mention in the *Begriffsschrift*. I think this works both ways, and some of the things he says about predicates reflect his thinking about the properties and relations to which they refer. Frege clearly had the idea that a sentence had a reference determined by the references of its parts. The word he uses most often is "*Umstand.*" "Circumstance" is the natural translation. The German word, like the English one, can be used for the proposition or possibility of a certain object having a given property, or for the event of its doing so, or for the surrounding of such an event. Circumstances and facts were important in nineteenth-century philosophy, as logicians and philosophers developed frameworks for dealing with relations without falling into idealism, but Frege does not mention this.[3]

Greatly simplified, Aristotle thought that subjects stood for objects, predicates for properties, and truth consisted in those objects having those properties. This does not work with relations. Two thousand years of thinking about that followed. Perhaps relations are an illusion. Perhaps there is really just one subject, of which everything is predicated; relation words are just methods for constructing ways of predicating properties of the Absolute.

Or perhaps relations are real. Facts are not exhausted by objects having properties; they also involve objects standing in relations. Possible facts are circumstances, complexes of relations and objects that might stand in them, and, in the limiting case, complexes of properties, unary relations, and objects that might have them. That is my view; it is more or less what Peirce and Russell came to think in working out the logic of relations, and I think it was the view Frege found natural when he wrote the *Begriffsschrift*.

But let me reiterate that in saying that in the *Begriffsschrift* Frege took sentences to refer to circumstances, my evidence is simply that he says

---

[3] See (Olson, 1987).

of various sentences that they refer to circumstances, not any detailed presentation of such a doctrine. It seems to me that there is a way of looking at things in the *Begriffsschrift*, which Frege found natural at this early stage of developing his ideas. The key concept is not circumstance, but *falling under*. When we say "Caesar conquered Gaul" we are saying that Caesar and Gaul fall under the first level concept of *conquers(x,y)*. When we say "Being a conquerer requires having an army" we are saying that the first level concepts of being a conquerer and having an army fall under the higher level concept of requiring. When we say "Caesar existed" it looks like we are saying that Caesar falls under the concept of existing, but that is confused. We are saying that the concept of *being Caesar* or *being identical with Caesar* falls under the higher level concept of being instantiated. Frege continues to speak of levels and falling under in later works, when he no longer talks about circumstances.

The idea of *falling under* raises some questions. Later, Frege was to draw a very sharp distinction between concepts and objects; concepts are *unsaturated* just as concept words are incomplete; objects are saturated, just as names, expressions for objects, are complete. And he required that functions generally, and concepts in particular, are to be defined on all objects if they are to be truly understood. If we have a definition of "larger than" that tells us for any two numbers n and m, whether n is larger than m, our work is not done. We also have to understand whether say, 17 is larger than Julius Caesar, and if not, why not. Then we have *falling under* itself; it seems to be a relation that holds between first level concepts and objects, and n level concepts and $n - 1$ level concepts. This combination of doctrines seems likely to lead to paradox. Russell posed his famous paradox in terms of the class that contains all classes not members of themselves. It can be restated in terms of concept under which all concepts fall that do not fall under themselves. But Frege does not address such worries in the *Begriffsschrift*, the *Grundlagen* or the 1890 Essays. They come up later.

Still, the following framework seems quite intuitive. At the bottom we have basic circumstances: an object falling under first level property, or objects falling under a first level relation: Caesar was Roman; Caesar conquered Gaul. Then we have circumstances in which an object and a first level property fall under an a complex second level property: Caesar had a nationality; some Roman conquered Gaul. Then we have structures in which first level properties fall under second level ones: Being Roman was a nationality; being Roman was a more common nationality than being Carthiginian. And so on. Concept-Writing gives us the tools to express all these structures and more. This structure, inexplicit as it was in the *Begriffsschrift*, was the semantical framework in the background of Frege's discovery, or invention, of first and second order logic. It lends itself naturally to development within a consistent typed theory; having said that, I will not worry about paradoxes here.

2.2 Quantification

Frege's treatment of predicates as functions was not merely an insight about how a language might better reflect logical structure. It was also connected with his watershed accomplishment, his analysis of what we now call "quantification." We now say that the variables in our predicates cannot only be replaced by names, to yield sentences, but can be "bound" by quantifiers. In English we can say "Caesar conquered Gaul," but also "Someone conquered Gaul." If we are stuck in the subject-predicate way of looking at things, we'll call "Someone" the subject-term, and wonder what it stands for. An indefinite person? A collection of persons? But we learn that the proper translation is "$\exists x$(Conquered Gaul x)." The x in the existential quanitifier *binds* the x that follows. This is all due to Frege, but it is not quite the way he put it.

In Frege's notation we translate an assertion of "Caesar conquered Gaul" as

$\vdash$ Conquered (*Caesar, Gaul*).

The initial heavy vertical line is the judgment stroke, the horizontal line that follows is the content stroke. Frege says that if we insist on finding the subject-predicate structure in the Concept-Writing, we can regard the vertical stroke as the predicate "is a fact" and the content, what follows the horizontal line, as the subject.

Content strokes do most of the scope-indicating work, rather than parentheses and brackets. Negation is indicated by vertical bars hanging from the content stroke, so "It is not the case that Caesar conquered Gaul" is

├────┬─ *Conquered* (*Caesar, Gaul*).

Frege introduced the universal quantifier, now usually symbolized as "(∀)". He did not have an existential quantifier like "(∃)" in his *Begriffsschrift*, but put negations on either side of a universal quantifier. So, "Everything conquered Gaul" is

├────ᵃ─ *Conquered* (*a, Gaul*).

and "Something conquered Gaul" is

├────┬──ᵃ──┬─ *Conquered* (*a, Gaul*).

The two-dimensional notation comes into Concept-Writing with conditionals. "If Caesar conquered Gaul, then he was a Roman" becomes

├──┬──── *Roman* (*Caesar*)
   │
   └──── *Conquered* (*Caesar, Gaul*)

Modern logicians do not find the content strokes useful; their work is done by parentheses and brackets. The judgement stroke more or less evolved into "⊢". Frege used Gothic letters with his quantifiers. He did not *bind* the variables in predicates, but replaced the place-holding variables with the Gothic letters from the quantifier. He also avoided the use of the term "variable," which he associated with various unpromising views about what variables stood for found in the history of logic; the term has now been stripped of such associations, which is not to imply that a consensus has been reached on what variables are. These are minor differences. The theory of quantification, the most important development in logic since the syllogism, is due in large part to Frege.

In the *Begriffsschrift* Frege provides us with the truth-conditions of Concept-Writing sentences in terms of the references of their parts by telling us which circumstances they stand for; the sentences are true if those circumstances are facts. This is what we now think of as "providing a semantics." Frege does not use this terminology. As noted, "falling under" is a key phrase. Caesar and Gaul falls under the concept of *Conquers*(*x, y*). Caesar falls under the concept *Man*(*x*). Thus saying that Caesar falls under the concept *Man*(*x*) is a way of saying Caesar has the property of being a man, and so the circumstance of Caesar's being a man is a fact. Properties also have properties; that is, they fall under higher order properties. The word "concept" is a bit more natural with the phrase "falling under." The property of being a flower is a botanical property; that is, the concept of being a flower falls under the concept of being a botanical concept. The concept of personal identity is examined by Hume; that is, it has the property of being examined by Hume; that is, it falls under the concept, being examined by Hume. Hume and the concept of personal identity stand in the relation that the first investigated the second; that is, the two entities fall under the relation *investigated(x,y)*. So we have objects falling under concepts, concepts falling under concepts, and so on. In each case we may or may or may not have a fact.

Frege emphasizes the difference between a concept falling under another concept and its being subsumed by another concept. The concept of being an animal *subsumes* the concept of being a human, which is to say all humans are animals. But the concept of being a human does not *fall under* the concept of being an animal; the concept of being a human is not an animal.

In modern set-theoretic terms, and confining ourselves to unary concepts, *a falls under b* comes to *a is in the extension of b*. So *a* can be a first level concept, in which case objects fall under it, or a higher level concept, in which case lower level concepts fall under it. *b subsumes a* comes to *the set of entities that fall under a is a subset of the entities that fall under b*. If *a subsumes b*, then all the entities that fall under *b* will also fall under *a*. I am human, so I am an animal. But the concept of being a human is not itself an animal. One must keep in mind that Frege did not think in modern set theoretic terms; as we shall see he had a different conception of extensions than we do now.

The subject-predicate picture is especially misleading with sentences that begin with an indefinite description, like "A gnat is a pest." The subject term is "a gnat". What sort of thing could that refer to? In Concept-Writing, we have

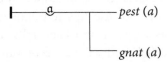

Thus we have two ways of going from incomplete expressions with variables—predicates or concept-words—to complete sentences. We can replace the variables in the predicates with names, or we can use eliminate them in favor of the gothic letters from a quantifier. In the latter case we are saying that the relevant concepts fall under higher level concepts.

To say that concepts fall under higher level concepts is to say that concepts themselves have properties. One important property that concepts have is their *marks*; that is, the properties that individuals (or lower level concepts) have to have, in order to fall under the concept in question. To be a human, one might suppose, requires having a heart and a kidney. So marks are naturally a bit confusing; they are properties of things falling under a concept. But that the concept having a kidney is a mark of the concept being human is a relation between concepts.

2.3 Conceptual Content in the *Begriffsschrift*

It is often assumed, because of Frege's own critique in "On Sense and Denotation," that the *Begriffsschrift* philosophy of language and his treatment of the identity problems were deeply flawed, the product of an "immature" phase of his career, as Dummett says (Dummett, 1973/81). Hans Sluga is an exception (Sluga, 1980). Frege's concepts of conceptual contents and circumstances are seldom taken very seriously. In contrast I think there are aspects of Frege's thought that are most easily understood by reference to the framework that seemed most natural to him when he designed Concept-Writing and invented first and second order logic. As interesting as Frege's later ideas were, and as voluminous the literature they have inspired, none has had the lasting influence on science that the *Begriffsschrift* has had. The idea that the ideas that led to it should be dismissed as "immature" is not plausible.

The central notion in the semantics of the *Begriffschrift* is *conceptual content*. Consider the statement "The Greeks defeated the Persians at Plataea." This describes a certain circumstance, and asserts that it occurred. Rewrite this as: It is a fact that the Persians were defeated by the Greeks at Plataea. In Concept-Writing, the job of "is a fact" is done by Frege's judgement sign, the vertical bar. The "that" corresponds to Frege's content sign, a horizontal bar, later just called "the horizontal."

The conceptual content is what we have left after we remove the judgement bar.

The conceptual content of a sentence is a *circumstance*, something that may or may not be a fact. The conceptual content of the whole sentence is determined by the conceptual contents of its parts. The conceptual content of a name expression is the object to which it refers. The conceptual content of a predicate is a property or relation, the condition that its arguments must meet for the sentence to be true.

In my terminology, first level circumstances consist of objects having properties and standing in relations—at a time and place if we are dealing with concrete objects. If the objects have the properties and stand in the relations, the circumstance is a fact. Higher level circumstances consist entirely of first level concepts falling under second level ones, or second level ones falling under third level ones. It is a second level fact, for example, that there are philosophers; that is, that *being a philosopher* falls under *being instantiated*, that is:

$$\vdash\!\!\!-\!\!-\!\!-\!\!\!\begin{array}{c}\alpha\\\top\end{array}\!\!-\!\!-\!\!\!\top\!\!- \quad \text{is a philosopher } (a).$$

I will usually use "circumstances" for first level circumstances, and "property-structures" for higher level circumstances. But when it is useful to emphasize the unity of the *Begriffsschrift* theory, with everything tied together by *falling under*, I will call them "higher level circumstances." I will do my best to make things clear on such occasions.

2.4 Carving up Circumstances?

Frege introduces his metaphor of carving up content in Section 64 of the the *Foundations of Arithmetic*:

> The judgement "line *a* is parallel to line *b*
>
>   *a // b*
>
> can be taken as an identity. If we do this, we obtain the concept of direction, and say: "the direction of line *a* is identical with the direction of line *b*??. Thus we replace the symbol // by the more generic symbol =,

through removing what is specific in the content of the former and dividing it between *a* and *b*. We carve up the content in a way different from the original way, and this yields us a new concept.

But a form of the carving up content thesis already emerges in the *Begriffsschrift*. Following Kit Fine (Fine, 1982) and Kenneth Olson (Olson, 1987), we can distinguish between two conceptions of circumstances and facts. I will call them "circumstances as happenings" and "circumstances as states of affairs." My working metaphysics, sort of a stew of Whitehead (Whitehead, 1929) and Frege, is that reality consists of happenings. Possibilities, including circumstances, Thoughts, and other conceptions of propositions, are abstract objects we use to deal with it. Humans think of and describe what happens mainly in terms of uniformities across happening: objects, properties, locations, and times. States of affairs and other possibilities are an adjunct to this this very basic conceptual equipment. They are abstract objects individuated by properties, objects, times, and locations. This is how I think of circumstances, and it is the concept of circumstances in which I am interpreting Frege's use of the term; the concept I am to a certain extent foisting on Frege.

The alternative is to think of facts not as states of affairs that happenings make factual, but as happenings themselves, the basic metaphysical building blocks of reality. A more natural word might be "events," but I think it has the same ambiguity as "circumstance." So I will just say "happenings." On this conception, we might use different objects and properties to describe the same happenings. In the spirit of Quine we might describe a given happening in terms of ducks crossing the street, or a temporal parts of ducks crossing temporal parts of streets, or in many other ways.

Fine calls these the "empirical" and "structuralist conceptions"; Olson substitutes "existential" for "empirical."

Frege never worries about duck parts. And, I have said, he does not tell us much about how he thinks of circumstances. But he explores different ways of carving up the same conceptual content. Perhaps, to explain what he had in mind, it would be useful to being in the conception of circumstances as happenings.

Frege tells us that the pair of sentences, "The Greeks defeated the Persians at Plataea" and "The Persians were defeated by the Greeks at Plataea" have the same conceptual content, even though the subjects and predicates differ. His main point is that subjects and predicates have no logical significance. Granting that, it seems that the relations of *defeating* and *being defeated by* are different relations, which is to say different functions. Indeed, it seems, extrapolating a bit from various things he says, he supposes that the following combinations of functions and arguments all have the same conceptual content, that is, yield the same circumstance as value:

Defeated (the Greeks, the Persians) = y
Defeated the Persians (the Greeks) = y
Were defeated by (the Persians, the Greeks) = y
Were defeated by the Greeks (the Persians) = y
Occurred (the defeat of the Persians by the Greeks) = y

If these different combinations of functions and arguments all yield the same value, the same circumstance, that of the Greeks having defeated the Persians, Frege did not have a straightforward conception of circumstances as states of affairs. This does not mean that he thought of them as happenings, only that, however he was thinking of them, my interpretation of Frege's circumstances as state of affairs is not the whole story. Still, in the *Begriffsschrift* Frege has a conception of the subject matter of a sentence that is not obliterated at the level of *Bedeutung*, as happens later in the theory of sense and denotation. In the series above, the Persians, the Greeks and defeating seem to be in some sense the basic subject matter. *Having the same basic subject matter* would be an equivalence relation on states of affairs. I will not work this into my account, however, as the added complexity would not add much for the purpose of understanding the *Begriffsschrift*, and the whole category of circumstances drops out in the theory of sense and denotaton. I will persist in my interpretation of circumstances as state of affairs until Chapter 7, by which time I will have developed an apparatus that allows me to say something about the issue that might be useful.

2.5 Content Problems

In Section 3 of the *Begriffsschrift*, Frege tells us that if sentences have the same conceptual content, they have the same logical consequences. As Warren Goldfarb (2010) cogently explains in his fine essay "Frege's Conception of Logic" (Goldfarb, 2010), Frege had a very straightforward view of logic, but one rather different than the view or views of logic that have developed since the works of Tarski and Gödel.

Goldfarb distinguishes between the *schematic* conception of logic, the standard modern view, and the *universalist* conception, Frege's view. Schemas are sentence forms constructed from quantifiers, truth-functional connectives, and schematic letters for predicates and names. Given a universe of discourse, we may assign the schematic letters various interpretations. A sentence schema is logically valid if any interpretation of it is true. This was not Frege's conception. He thought that logic, like any science, consists of truths, at least in its finished state. It differs from other sciences in being the most general. He thought that the truths of logic were *analytic*, in (more or less) Kant's sense. If we understand them—which may require a lot of work—we will see that they are true, without having to consult what is going on in the world. To see that two sentences have the same content—have the same consequences—one may have to put in a lot of work developing a proof of this fact. But one should not have to go outside one's study to establish empirical facts.

Circumstances simply do not provide contents that meet these criteria. This is what Frege's identity problems showed.

3

Frege's *Begriffsschrift*: Problems

I distinguish four identity problems. The first two are implicitly considered in the *Begriffsschrift* and involve identity sentences. The third problem involves reflexive relations other than identity; Frege does not discuss it. The fourth problem only comes up much later, in "Function and Concept." It involves identity, but not identity sentences, and it seem likely that it was instrumental in moving Frege from the *Begriffsschrift* theory to the theory of sense and denotation, although he does not say so. I will use an example that has become standard in discussions of Frege:

(4)   Hesperus = Hesperus

(5)   Hesperus = Phosphorus

In fact "Hesperus" and "Phosphorus" were ancient names for the planet Venus. So (5) is true as well as (4). This means that there is only one heavenly object involved. Hence, both sentences refer to the same circumstance. But they do not pass the test for having the same conceptual content. Example (4) is trivial, analytic or nearly so. Example (5) conveys information that the Ancients did not have. More importantly, they do not pass the inference test for having the same content. One can infer (6) from (5), but not from (4):

(6)   "Hesperus" and "Phosphorus" refer to the same thing.

I call this the "Name Problem." The second problem arises if one has associated "ways of determination" with these names. Suppose "Hesperus" is standardly introduced by pointing to the first planet to appear in the evening sky and saying "That is Hesperus." "Phosphorus" is standardly introduced by pointing to the last planet to disappear from the morning sky and saying, "That is Phosphorus." Then one can learn something

Frege's Detour: An Essay on Meaning, Reference, and Truth. John Perry, Oxford University Press (2019).
© John Perry DOI: 10.1093/oso/9780198812821.001.0001

significant from (5) one cannot learn from (4), the information the Ancients lacked:

(7)   The first planet to appear in the evening sky is the last planet to disappear from the morning sky.

So (5), together with the ways of determination associated with the names, leads not only to the inference about co-reference, but also to a more substantial bit of information. Example (4), with the same additional premises, does not lead to (7). Again, conceptual content, conceived in terms of circumstances, does not meet the inference criterion for sameness of content.

I call this the "Co-instantiation Problem." Frege deals with both problems in the *Begriffsschrift*. His solution involves replacing "=" with his new symbol, "≡", so we have instead of (4) and (5):

(8)   Hesperus ≡ Hesperus

(9)   Hesperus ≡ Phosphorus

Contrary to appearance, (8) and (9) are statements about names, to the effect that they refer to the same thing. So their conceptual contents are not the same; the circumstances referred to involve the names themselves, and not the planet they refer to.

The third problem I call "Wilson's Problem." George Wilson pointed out in a Cornell Colloquium in 1967 that sentences that involve reflexive relations other than identity also raise problems that Section 8 cannot handle. If we know that there is a planet called "Hesperus," we will know that "Hesperus is the same size as Hesperus" is true. But, without additional information, we will not know that "Hesperus is the same size as Phosphorus" is true. Frege does not notice this problem in the *Begriffsschrift*, or anywhere else that I know of.

Frege's fourth problem is not discussed in the *Begriffsschrift*; Frege brings it up 12 years later in "Function and Concept":

If we say "The Evening Star is a planet with a shorter period of revolution than the Earth," the Thought we express is not the same one we express with "The Morning Star is a planet with a shorter period of revolution than the Earth." Someone who does not know that the Morning Star is the Evening Star might regard one as true and the other as false. (FC, 138)

The example does not involve identity sentences, and so is not handled by Frege's *Begriffsschrift* solution. I will use a simpler example:

(10) Hesperus is moonless.

(11) Phosphorus is moonless.

Examples (10) and (11) refer to the same circumstance, that Venus is moonless. So they have the same conceptual content. But then they should have the same consequences. But they do not. From (10) one can logically infer "if a planet has any moons, it is not Hesperus." But that does not follow from (11). Co-referring names make the same contribution to conceptual content, if the conceptual content of a sentences is a circumstance. So replacement of one by another should not affect what follows from a sentence. But it does.

I will call this the "General Problem."

3.1 Background Fable

In discussing Frege's identity problems, in both the *Begriffsschrift* and the 1890 Essays, it will be helpful to have a stock of examples that will provide a sort of common currency for points Frege makes and points I wish to make. They will be based on a fable I now present. I use the names "Hesperus" and "Phosphorus" to illustrate the problems, rather than the letters "a" and "b", and "A" and "B" as Frege does, since I think it is helpful to have real names before us. Frege eventually uses "the morning star" and "the evening star," which he calls names, to illustrate his problems with identity. But these look like inaccurate definite descriptions, since the "stars" turned out not to be stars, but the planet Venus. Somewhere along the line, the names "Hesperus" and "Phosphorus" became the more or less standard way to explain Frege's problems, and I will join this tradition.

So we start with this pair of sentences:

(4)   Hesperus = Hesperus

(5)   Hesperus = Phosphorus

Whatever the facts of ancient history, or the role of ways of determination and senses in language, in my fable things work the way Frege thought they should. We take "Hesperus" to be the ancient Babylonian name for the first heavenly object, other than the sun or the moon, to appear in the evening sky, and "Phosphorus" to be the ancient Babylonian name for the last heavenly object, other than the sun or the moon, to disappear from the morning sky. These objects are in fact both the planet Venus.

To simplify things a bit, I pretend that "Hesperus" and "Phosphorus" came into their language at a time when the Babylonians realized that the heavenly bodies prominent in the morning and evening skies were planets, not stars, but before they realized they were the same planet. The term "Hesperus" was first introduced, and then explicitly taught, by pointing to the first planet to appear in the night sky. And "Phosphorus" was similarly assigned to the last planet to disappear in the morning sky. So what Frege calls "senses" in "On Sense and Denotation" and "ways of determination" in the *Begriffsschrift* are definitely associated with *these* names.

Then, in my story, a brilliant Babylonian made a discovery that she announced with (5):

(5)   Hesperus = Phosphorus

It seems that the Babylonians learned *two* things from (5) that Frege's *Begriffsschrift* theory would not account for without Section 8. First, the Name Problem: the names "Hesperus" and "Phosphorus" refer to the same object. Second, the Co-instantiation Problem: that the properties of being the first planet to appear in the evening (for short: being the evening planet) and the last planet to disappear in the morning (for short: being the morning planet) are co-instantiated. Since (4) and (5) refer to the same circumstance, that Venus is Venus, and so have the same conceptual content, neither bit of learning seems to be explained by the basic theory without Section 8.

One further wrinkle will be helpful. Edwina is a precocious Babylonian child. She hears the exciting new discovery, "Hesperus = Phosphorus" before her parents have taken her out in the evening and morning and taught her the ways of determination associated with these words. For all she knows, "Hesperus" and "Phosphorus" could be names of pet birds, or children, or streets in Baghdad, the new town down the road. She does not learn anything about astronomy. But soon after that her parents do their duty, taking her out in the evening and morning, and Edwina learns that the way of determination associated with "Hesperus" is being the first planet to appear in the evening, and that the way of determination associated with "Phosphorus" is being the last planet to disappear in the morning. From this, together with what she *already* learned from hearing "Hesperus = Phosphorus," Edwina learns a substantial astronomical fact, that the first planet to appear in the evening is the last planet to disappear in the morning. She would not have learned this from simply knowing "Hesperus = Hesperus." With all that in mind, return to our example, and the first problem it presents, the Name Problem.

(4)   Hesperus = Hesperus

(5)   Hesperus = Phosphorus

Example (5) is true, since both "Hesperus" and "Phosphorus" turn out to refer to to the planet Venus. Then both sentences refer to to the same circumstance and have the same conceptual content, that Venus is identical with Venus. But one can learn from (5), but not from (4) it seems, that the names "Hesperus" and "Phosphorus" refer to the same thing. Something seems to have gone wrong.

3.2 Section 8 of the *Begriffsschrift*

It seems that the job of Section 8 of the *Begriffsschrift* is to solve the first two problems. But there is a rather annoying exegetical problem here. Frege does not tell us, in the *Begriffsschrift*, that he is bothered by the Name problem. The sign "=" occurs in sections 1 and 5 of the book, before the introduction of "≡", and never again. In "On Sense and Denotation," Frege says that in the *Begriffsschrift* he thought that identity was a relation between names, not things. But he does not say that, or give any sign that he thinks that, in the *Begriffsschrift*. He carefully distinguishes between identity, a relation between a thing and itself and no other thing, and *identity of content*, a relation between names. It is a relation that names have when their *contents* — that is, the objects they refer to — are *identical*, in the ordinary uncontroversial sense of there being just one thing.

The description of the *Begriffsschrift* Frege gives in the opening paragraph of "On Sense and Denotation" is more informative about "On Sense and Denotation" than it is about *Begriffsschrift*; we'll discuss it when we turn to that essay. But I think it is fair to take it to show *something* about how Frege remembered his motivations in the *Begriffsschrift*, in particular that the Name Problem illustrated by (4) and (5) *was* bothering him, even though he did not say so, and produced no such examples. Otherwise, the motivation for Section 8 of the *Begriffsschrift* remains a bit of a mystery.

Frege starts the section with no mention of identity, and no use of "=", but rather an explanation of the relation he calls "identity of content" (*Inhaltsgleichheit*). The symbol he introduces for it, "≡", requires the names that flank it to refer to themselves. Once Frege has introduced "≡", "=" disappears from the *Begriffsschrift*; he uses "≡" where we might have expected "=". An important instance is Section 20, the *Begriffsschrift* version of Leibniz's Principle of Identity. We usually express this principle with '=', as Frege did later in Section 50 of the *Grundgesetze*:

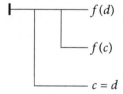

But in the *Begriffsschrift*, Frege uses "≡":

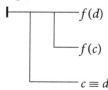

It seems that Frege's problem, as he diagnosed it when he wrote the *Begriffsschrift*, was not with identity, but with "=".[1]

We can perhaps get a sense of the problem by staring at the first version while thinking of conceptual contents as circumstances. We need to bracket any relevant ideas from later developments in logic, in particular model theory. If "=" refers to identity, then "$c = d$" asserts that a certain object is self-identical; that is the circumstance involved. But if "$c = d$" is true, the very same circumstance would be involved if we had "$c = c$" or "$d = d$" as the first antecedent. But then we clearly could not infer "$f(d)$". We have not changed the conceptual content of the first antecedent since we have not changed the circumstance. But we have changed its inferential power.

It seems that what we are doing, when we make this inference, is replacing the name "c" in the the antecedent with the name "d" in the consequent. So if the inference we are making is correct, "$c = d$" must be giving us the information about names, the information that "c" and "d" refer to the same thing. But that is not what "=" means! At least it is not what it is supposed to mean. If "=" really means what it supposed to mean, identity, perhaps it is not really the symbol we need. Instead, we need a symbol for something that is closely related to identity, namely, the relation between names that refer to the same object, that is, to the *identical* thing. We need a symbol for *identity of content*, and should probably just retire "=".

That is my best guess as to how Frege was thinking of things. But he does not tell us that this is the thinking that led to his introduction of "≡". And there is nothing in what he does tell us that explains *why* we should have misinterpreted "=" in this way. I will call this misinterpretation the "mystery step." He starts Section 8 by justifying the need for a sign for identity of content, without mentioning "=" or the mystery step.

Whereas in other contexts signs are merely representatives of their content, so that every combination into which they enter expresses only

---

[1] Both principles are often called called "Leibniz's Law." The first version above is more accurately called the Principle of the Indiscernibility of the Identical, a metaphysical principle about identity, objects, and properties, which Leibniz clearly held. It must not be confused with his famous and controversial principle of the Identity of Indiscernibles. The second version above is basically a rather unusual formulation of the principle that permits substitution.

a relation between their respective contents, they suddenly display their own selves when they are combined by means of the sign for identity of content, for it expresses the circumstance that two names have the same content. Hence the introduction of a sign for identity of content necessarily produces a bifurcation in the meaning of all signs: they stand at times for their content, at times for themselves. (Section 8)

Frege does not give us an explanation of what is going on with identity sentences like (4) and (5) in Section 8. Rather, he gives us a new symbol for what it seems we often gather from sentences like (5), and often wish to convey with them. So we can distinguish between (4) and (5), neither of which tell us anything about names, and

(8)   Hesperus ≡ Hesperus

(9)   Hesperus ≡ Phosphorus

one of which tells us something quite trivial about one name, the other tells us something more important about two of them. There is no mystery that (8) and (9) have different content. They do not stand for the same circumstance. They are not about Venus. They are about the names "Hesperus" and "Phosphorus" and the relation of co-reference.

As I said, on this interpretation, there is a "mystery step" in Frege's account. *Why* do (4) and (5) get misused and misinterpreted so as to convey (8) and (9)? Examples (4) and (5) have the same conceptual content. How can a semantically competent hearer get different information from them? Or why does it at least seem that she can? Frege gives an account of where the mystery step ends up — with (8) and (9). But he does not explain why we end up in different places, when we seem to be starting from the same place — that is, with the conceptual content common to (4) and (5).

Having explained identity of content, Frege asks what the point of having two names for the same thing might be, which leads him to the second problem mentioned in Chapter 2, the Co-instantiation problem.

At first we have the impression that what we are dealing with pertains merely to the *expression* and *not to the thought*, that we do not need different signs at all for the same content and hence no sign whatsoever for identity of content. To show that this is an empty illusion I take the following example from geometry. Assume that on the circumference of a circle there is a fixed point A about which a ray revolves. When this ray passes through the center of the circle, we call the other point at which it intersects the circle the point B associated with this position of the ray. The point of intersection, other than A, of the ray and the circumference will then be called the point B associated with the position of the ray at any time; this point is such that continuous variations in its position must always correspond to continuous variations in the point of the ray. Hence the name B denotes something indeterminate so long as the corresponding position of the ray has not been specified. We can now ask: what point is associated with the position of the ray when it is perpendicular to the diameter? The answer will be: the point A. In this case, therefore, the name B has the same content as has the name A; and yet we could not have used only one name from the beginning, since the justification for that is given only by the answer. One point is determined in two ways: (1) immediately through intuition and (2) as a point B associated with the ray perpendicular to the diameter.

Here is a diagram borrowed from Peter Geach showing the construction Frege had in mind.

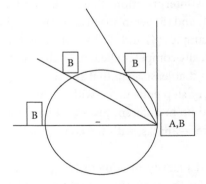

Frege here anticipates his later concepts of mode of presentation and sense; we have two ways of determining the same point, one associated with A and the other with B. Thus we gain useful information from "A ≡ B," not just information about the "A" and "B".

3.3 Virtues of Frege's *Begriffsschrift* Solution

Frege rejected his own *Begriffsschrift* solution in "On Sense and Denotation" and it would be difficult to find praise for it from other philosophers. I think it deserves more credit.

It seems indisputable that we do learn facts about expressions from identity statements, and these facts can be quite useful, perhaps not on their own, but in combination with other facts. And that seems often to be the intent of such statements. At a party, I tell you, "That man is Fred." I want you to learn that the person I refer to as "that man" has the name "Fred." It should be useful to know this when interacting with him, and will be handy way for you to store knowledge about him in your mind when he is no longer present. Or imagine that you are going to visit San Sebastian in the Basque Country. But you cannot find it on the map of the Basque Country hanging on my wall. I tell you, "San Sebastian is Donostia." You will certainly learn that the names co-refer. On Frege's theory, as I have presented it, you interpret my remark as "Donostia ≡ San Sebastian," and I intend for you to do this. So interpreted, I convey this is by referring to the two names, and predicating the the relation of co-signification. So the Name problem is solved, at least given the mystery step.

And where names are associated with ways of determination, it also solves the Co-instantiation problem. From staring at the map, you had associated *being the capital city of Gipuzkoa* with "Donostia." From your reading, you had associated *being the site of the famous beach, Playa de la Concha* with "San Sebastian." So when you learn that Donostia ≡ San Sebastian, you also learn that the site of the famous beach is the capital city of Gipuzkoa.

3.4 Shortcomings of Frege's *Begriffsschrift* Solution

There are, however, serious shortcomings with Frege's account, so interpreted. First there is the Name Problem and the mystery step. How does one get from (5) to (9)? The introduction of "≡" identifies *what* we learn, but does not explain *how* we learn it, given that the circumstance to which

(5) refers does not involve names. Retiring the "=" symbol does not seem to solve the problem, but simply to shield us from it.

Second, retiring the "=" symbol neither solves nor even shields us from Wilson's problem.

Given that we somehow get from "=" to "≡", Frege does offer a solution to the Co-Instantiation Problem, more or less the solution he provides in his theory of sense and denotation.

Third, the General Problem is not considered much less solved. The *Begriffsschrift* account works at most for identity sentences. But as Frege points out in "Function and Concept," the problem seems to have to do with *identity in general*, not merely identity sentences. Consider again,

(10)   Hesperus is moonless.

(11)   Phosphorus is moonless.

(10) and (11) are not identity sentences, and so cannot be replaced with versions containing "≡" to explain their difference in cognitive significance. Oddly, Frege does not mention this problem with his *Begriffsschrift* solution in his critique at the beginning of "On Sense and Denotation."

Given Wilson's Problem and the General Problem, nothing in Section 8 resolves the fundamental lack of fit between Frege's inference criterion for sameness of content and his choice of circumstances as the contents of sentences. In the *Begriffsschrift* Frege identified a particular subset of problems connected with the fact that circumstances, however exactly or inexactly he may have been thinking of them, do not fit with his general criterion for sameness of content. The problems involved "=". But by the time of his 1890 Essays he had recognized that the problem generalizes. The problem has to do with identity, not with the identity sign. Or more accurately, it has to do with circumstances. Circumstances simply do not get at the truth-conditions of sentences in a way that captures their cognitive significance. They need to be replaced with something that captures the conditions that objects must satisfy to be referred to by the expressions that the speaker uses and the hearer understands. This is the job senses will perform in the 1890 Essays. Thus the *Begriffsschrift* leaves things in a rather unsatisfactory state with respect to the identity problems and with the nature of the contents of sentences. The mystery step is unexplained. And the theory does not extend to Wilson's problem or the general problem, the difference in content between (10) and (11).

3.5 Circumstances and Understanding

Let us return to our Babylonians. Dan the Astronomer announces that Hesperus is moonless. He says, "Hesperus is moonless." (Recall that for unexplained reasons my Babylonians spoke English.) They all believe him, and come to know that Hesperus is moonless. Why are not circumstances helpful in understanding it? Here are the major points that seem to lead to this conclusion:

The expression "Hesperus" is associated by the conventions and practices of language with the property of being the first planet visible in the night sky, and the expression "is moonless" is associated with the property of having no moons. The property associated with "Hesperus" is *graspable*. On a clear evening, at any rate, one experiences seeing the first planet (the ones that do not twinkle) become visible.

The Babylonians grasped what a moon is; it is being one of *those* (pointing to our moon). Having a moon is a property a planet has if it has such a moon, related to it as earth's is to it. It seems like there is a reasonably graspable property associated with "is moonless." So, with "Hesperus is moonless" they associate the Thought that the first planet to appear in the evening sky has no moons.

This means that what they grasp, what they understand, is *not* captured by the circumstance that Venus is moonless. Being moonless is one condition that the denotation of "Hesperus" must satisfy for the sentence to be true. But it also must satisfy the condition of being the evening planet. So it is a mistake consider the circumstance that Venus has no moons to be what Dan discovered and told everyone. The circumstance simply does not do what is required; it does not get at *how* Dan and the Babylonians *thought of* the planet. But this is an essential part of describing what he discovered and they all learned.

This is more obvious when we add that after a lot of morning investigations, Dan announced, "Phosphorus has a moon." He was of course mistaken. If we use circumstances to get at what he discovered and announced, it will sound like he was irrational; he announced that Venus was moonless and that it had a moon. But here first level circumstances are getting in the way. As long as we stick to higher level circumstances, the difference is clear. He believed that the evening planet had no moons, and he believed, quite consistently, that the morning planet had a moon; the first belief was true, the second false.

This is not to say that Venus is irrelevant. It is the planet Dan was investigating that has the property of being moonless and lacks the property of having a moon. Nor is identity of no interest. Hesperus *is* Phosphorus; that is something Dan *did not* know. But the importance of objects in general and Venus in particular does not need first level circumstances to be recognized. Particular objects are needed to *instantiate* properties. The higher-level circumstances involve existential quantification (as we now call it). For "Hesperus is moonless" to be true, an object is required; there has to be a planet that is the first one to appear in the evening, and it must have no moons. And circumstances are not needed to capture the conditions of the important identity that Hesperus is Phosphorus; it is simply the truth that there is a planet that instantiates both being the morning planet and being the evening planet.

On my interpretation, the Thoughts of the theory of sense and denotation are basically higher level circumstances, structures of properties falling under higher level properties. As Thoughts, their duties are better defined. They have to supply both the truth-conditions and cognitive significance of sentences. First level circumstances are stripped of both duties and sent into exile. Thoughts continue to acquire more duties, or at least have their duties clarified, through Frege's last writings about senses, where he emphasizes that they constitute a Third Realm, timeless and unchanging.

So here is my picture of the fate of first level circumstances in Frege's theory. The *Begriffsschrift* problems eventually made it clear to Frege that the circumstance referred to by a sentence did not capture everything necessary to understand the cognitive significance of the sentence or the full conditions required for its truth. A circumstance brings in *some* properties, those that are part of the circumstance. But identity problems made it clear that the *identifying* properties associated with expressions have to be brought in to account for their cognitive significance. Hence the senses of proper names, and the realm of Thoughts. Thoughts do not change intrinsically. Frege recognized that they change extrinsically, by being grasped. It seems to me that they change in a second way; they are made true various times in virtue of events in the mental and physical realms; once they have a truth value, they retain it.

Frege does not draw this conclusion, but I think he should have. He says that Thoughts have their truth values eternally. It seems that if a sentence is ever made true, it will never be made false and vice versa. So we could define "be true" as "has been, is now, or will be made true." Then we could say of each sentence it either be true or be false, and perhaps can add "eternally". That would allow us to use two-valued logic, without denying what seems plain to me, that many sentences are made true at times by events. But there is not evidence that Frege is thinking of things in this way. Without such an interpretation, Thoughts having their truth values eternally seems leave the physical and mental realms with little to do except to fit into the eternal framework ordained by the eternal truth values of Thoughts.

4

Sense and Denotation: The Theory

Frege presented his theory of sense and denotation in the 1890 Essays. "Function and Concept" was published in 1891, followed by "On Sense and Denotation" and "On Concept and Object" in 1892. He wrote an essay he did not publish, "Comments on *Sinn und Bedeutung*," at about this time, and sent a helpful letter to Husserl in 1891. Later, after publishing the *Grundgesetze* and trying to deal with Russell's paradox, he returned to developing his theory of senses and Thoughts, particularly in his *Logical Investigations*, written late in life.

In his later *Logical Investigations*, particularly "The Thought," Frege tells us more about senses and Thoughts, something about the metaphysics behind them. What he says is consistent with what he tells us in the 1890 Essays, but goes beyond what he says there in various ways. My working assumption is that the basic ideas of the *Logical Essays* were already present, if not all worked out, in the 1890s.

In "The Thought," Frege recognizes three Realms, the physical, the mental, and the "Third Realm," of senses and Thoughts. Causation is limited to the first two realms. The Third Realm is intrinsically unchanging. However, Thoughts in the Third Realm have at least one contingent, external relation to the other two. Frege recognizes that at various times minds *grasp* senses and Thoughts. This is what happens when we surmise that something might be the case, or come to believe that it is the case. As I mentioned above, it seems that Frege should also recognize there should a second sort of extrinsic change: Thoughts are *made true* by events in the other Realms that occur at various times. But he says that Thoughts are eternally true or false.

In this chapter I provide an account of the theory, as developed in the 1890 Essays, but using later work to suggest how he might deal with various things that are not discussed there. In the next chapter I focus on

Frege's Detour: An Essay on Meaning, Reference, and Truth. John Perry, Oxford University Press (2019).
© John Perry DOI: 10.1093/oso/9780198812821.001.0001

"On Sense and Denotation," and his argument for indirect denotation which leads to the Detour.[1]

4.1 Frege's New Scheme

Frege provided a summary of his theory in his 1891 letter to Husserl ((Beaney, 1997) 149–50), with basically this schema (Table 4.1):[2]

Table 4.1 Frege's Schema of Sense and Denotation from 1891 Husserl Letter (Beaney, 1997)

proper name	concept word		sentence
↓	↓		↓
sense of the proper name	sense of the concept word		sense of the sentence (thought)
↓	↓		↓
Bedeutung of the proper name (object)	[*Bedeutung* of the concept word] → (concept)	object falling under the concept	*Bedeutung* of the sentence (truth-value)

Introducing his theory of sense and denotation in "On Sense and Denotation," Frege makes it sound like he is simply *adding* a new level of senses:

> It is natural, now, to think of there being connected with a sign (name, combination of words, letter), besides that to which the sign denotes, which may be called the denotation of the sign, also what I would like to call the sense of the sign, wherein the mode of presentation is contained. ((Frege, 1960a), 59)

But this is misleading, for the level of *Bedeutung* is also changed. Table 4.2 is a schema he might have produced for the *Begriffsschrift*:

---

[1] After the 1890 Essays Frege focussed on his *Grundgesetze*. By the time the second volume was published in 1903, Russell had informed Frege of his paradox, which showed that Axiom V of the *Grundgesetze* had to be abandoned. After some efforts to deal with the paradox, Frege returned to the topic of senses in lectures he did not publish but for which we have Carnap's notes (Carnap, 2004). After the first world war, Frege published the three essays that comprise the *Logical Investigations*, in which he further developed his concepts of senses and Thoughts.

[2] I use "sentence" as a translation of "satz", change the order of the columns, and use brackets instead of braces in the concept-word column.

Table 4.2 Schema for *Begriffsschrift*

proper name	concept word	sentence
↓	↓	↓
Bedeutung of the	*Bedeutung* of the	*Bedeutung* of the
proper name	concept word	sentence
(object)	(concept)	(circumstance)

There are three changes. First, there are two rows below the expressions, for sense and *Bedeutung*, rather than simply one for *Bedeutung*. Second, for the *Bedeutung* of sentence we no longer have a circumstance, but a truth-value. Third, the account of *Bedeutung* for concept words has become rather complicated, as indicated by the extra column, the brackets, and the horizontal arrow.

4.2 What Are Senses and Thoughts?

Frege's theory of sense and denotation replaces his theory of conceptual content. The level of sense is added, and the level of *Bedeutung* changes signficantly. Still it seems that there is a certain continuity between the earlier and later theories. The level of sense seems to promote the *ways of determination* of the *Begriffsschrfit* to fill a central need in the theory, once the inadequacy of ≡ to solve the identity problems has been appreciated. while Thoughts seem to be conceptual contents without objects. This fits my interpretation, so that is where I will begin.[3]

As I said, on my interpretation, senses and Thoughts are basically the property structures of the *Begriffsschrift*, with their duties better articulated. The different ways of identifying objects are brought into the theory of content, replacing the objects that were constituents of circumstances. Objects, abstract or concrete, are not constituents of Thoughts, although the Thoughts themselves are objects. Ordinary objects remain in the theory, as the denotations of names. But they do not capture aspects of the cognitive significance contributed by expressions. That is the job

---

[3] Frege's Thoughts are not sets, and quite unlike sets of possible worlds. For a contemporary theory that, it seems to me, captures a great deal of Frege's picture, see Edward Zalta's theory of abstract objects in (Zalta, 1983).

of the senses that are associated, by the conventions and practices of a language, with the expressions.

On Frege's view, the relation of denotation, between a name and an object, its denotation, is *indirect*, in that the name is associated with a sense, a simple or complex property, that at most one object can have. The expression *has* the sense. The denotation is the unique object, if there is one, that *falls under* the sense. Expressions can have senses without having denotations, as in fiction, but this should be avoided in languages suitable for science.

Let's return to our Babylonians: "Phosphorus" has the sense *being the last planet to disappear from the morning sky*, while "Hesperus" has the sense *being the first planet to appear in the evening sky*. For the time being, we'll just take the sense of "is moonless" to be *having no moons*. When we combine these senses, we obtain two different truth-conditions for (10) and (11):

(10)   Hesperus is moonless.
   – Truth-conditions of (10): *That there is a unique object that is the first planet to appear in the evening sky and it is moonless.*

(11)   Phosphorus is moonless.
   – Truth-conditions of (11): *That there is a unique object that is the last planet to disappear from the morning sky and it is moonless.*

These fine-grained truth-conditions correspond to Thoughts. These are the contents that correspond to beliefs, and so serve as the *cognitive significance* of (10) and (11). They do the job circumstances did not do.

In identifying the conditions senses impose on the objects that fall under them, Frege uses descriptions. But I think this is a bit misleading. We imagine our Babylonian children as being able to pick out the planet they see in the morning and being aware that they are seeing the same planet morning after morning. We do not need to suppose that they have some articulated combination of ideas, captured by the sense of the description "the last planet to disappear from the morning sky" in order to identify and re-identify Phosphorus, and be in a position to learn its name. What grounds these abilities may be certain types of experiences that they have on many mornings; similarity among these experiences grounds their identification and re-identification. This is not to say that either the sense or its denotation is an experience, something subjective. It simply requires that an object can recognized, via its objective visible properties, even if one has no name for it. This is not something Frege emphasizes in the 1890 Essays, but it seems to be in the spirit of his later work on sense. It seems that the such a child will grasp a sense not as a sense *of* an expression, but as an objective property that is experienced not only by them but by others. And of course this happens to adults. I see an object with an unusual color and ask, "What's the name of that color." The term "mode of presentation," and Frege's emphasis on diagrams in illustrating his theory (Macbeth, 2005) indicate that, in spite of his insistence that ideas are subjective and not eligible to be senses, that he saw the connection between objective senses and experience.

One might ask, are these property structures really *all* there is to truth-conditions? Do not circumstances *also* supply truth-conditions? I think Frege's response would be that these Thoughts are all we *need*; circumstances, if they remain in his ontology at all, are merely derivative, coarse-grained ways of getting at truth-conditions, and serve no theoretical purpose.

We can motivate this point of view with a little bit of theology. This is not intended as an expression of my religious beliefs, nor a theory about Frege's, or anyone else's for that matter. Suppose by Wednesday of Creation Week, God has settled on the laws of logic (if such a decision was needed), and also on what properties and relations She wants instantiated in the world She is going to create. She has also, with her rather large mental capacity, considered all possible ways these properties and relations could be instantiated and co-instantiated. On Thursday, She considers all the alternatives, and settles on the one She likes best. Question: on Friday, does She have to decide *which* objects will do the instantiating? Or can She just say, with her favorite in mind, "Let it Be!" It seems the latter. Until the world is created, there are no objects to choose among. Bringing a world into existence that satisfies the chosen pattern of instantiation will take care of the objects.

As I said, I'm not trying to convert anyone to this theology; I'm simply trying to suggest a point of view that fits with what seems to be Frege's metaphysical point of view. Perhaps if our God cannot make a decision, and finally just says, "Let them all be" we have a theology that fits with

David Lewis's view of a rather high number of equally real possible worlds, sharing no concrete objects.

4.3 Concept Words

The interpretation so far is oversimplified. When it was first translated, some early readers of "On Sense and Denotation" were not sure that Frege drew the sense/denotation distinction for predicates; he barely mentions concepts in the essay. But Frege certainly drew the sense/denotation distinction for concept words as well as names, as the Husserl diagram (see Figure 4.1, 63) shows. In "Comments on *Sinn und Bedeutung*" he provides an the example of "conic section" and "curve of the second degree." A conic section is a figure formed by the intersection of a plane and a right circular cone. Depending on the angle of the plane with respect to the cone, a conic section may be a circle, an ellipse, a parabola, or a hyperbola. Descartes realised that a second degree equation generates a conic section in a Cartesian plane. It is certainly possible for someone —me, for example — to have spent most of his life believing that a circle is a conic section, but not believing that a circle is a curve of second degree — perhaps having been a bit un-attentive in an analytic geometry course.

This suggests that our treatment of (10) and (11) is too simple. Like "Hesperus" and "Phosphorus," the predicate "is moonless" also has a sense and a denotation. The property of being moonless is the denotation. What is the sense?

Our Babylonian children no doubt have noticed the moon many times, before they were taught the word "moon." They saw the moon; they associated a certain experience or range of experiences with seeing the moon, without having a name for the object they were seeing. They assumed that others had similar experiences, and that they were encountering an aspect of objective reality. When they are taught "moon" they associate the name with the moon via these experiences. The moon is the object I see many evenings. From there they perhaps have to learn that they are seeing the same object when they see circles and crescents. Eventually they have a sense to associate with "being moonless" that does not simply amount to "having no moons," but terminates in types of senses gained from experience. Frege does not spell anything like this out in the 1890

Essays, but perhaps suggests it when he returns to the topic of senses later in his career.

Remember that my Babylonians were pretty sophisticated. They knew that Hesperus and Phosphorus were planets, and that the earth was too. So, by the time that a Babylonian child is told and understands "Phosphorus is moonless" she perhaps will have a sense associated with the predicate "x has a moon" something like x is a planet that has the property the earth has, that I experience as there being something in the sky, especially at night, as having various shapes, from round to crescent. And like names, predicates might have senses without having denotations, like "being mimsy" or "being a borogrove." It seems that the Thought expressed by a sentence with a name will contain an existential quantifier. I should say it will contain a property that would be expressed in Concept Writing with a universal quantifier with negations on either side, but I will just mean that when I say a Thought contains and existential quantifier. Above, I said that the truth-conditions of (10) corresponding the truth-conditions of the Thought it expresses were:

That there is a unique object that is the first planet to appear in the evening sky and it is moonless.

It seems then that to express fully the Thought determined by (10) we need two existential quantifiers, something like:

That there is a unique object x and there is a unique property ϕ, such that x is the first planet to appear in the evening sky and ϕ is the property of being a planet that has something the property the earth has, that I experience as there being something in the sky, especially at night, as having various shapes, from round to crescent, and x does not have ϕ.

When we consider what I learned when I realized that being a conic section and being curve of second degree were the same property, this seems plausible. The Thought I came to believe would be expressed as:

There is a property ϕ of being curve formed by a cone intersecting with a plane and there is a property ψ of being a curve determined by a second degree polynomial equation in x and y, and ϕ and ψ are the same property.

There is a complication. We cannot say "$\phi = \psi$." Frege insists that identity is a relation that only holds between objects, not concepts. He does allow, however, that we can say that concepts are "the same" – but we have to be careful. We'll return to this below.

There does seem to be a bit of a problem here, however. Whatever we eventually decide about the phenomenon of reference, it does not seem all that implausible to suppose that truth-conditions of "Caesar was a Roman" really contains an existential quantifier. Russell thought so too, as different as his overall theory was from Frege's. The so-called "Frege-Russell" theory of names seemed to be accepted by most philosophers until the "New Theory of Reference" emerged in the 1970s, and is still favored by many.

But when it comes to properties, things do not seem so intuitive, especially taking into account the doctrine of indirect reference. If I say "All red things are colored things," it seems that the Thought I express is that everything that has the property of being red also has the property of being colored. But the Thought I really express is a bit more complicated. Let S_R be the sense I associate with "is red" and S_C be the sense I associate with "is colored." The Thought seems to be that there is a property determined by S_C and a property determined by S_C, and that everything that has the first has the second.

It seems more natural that what I said or believed is the instantiation of this property structure to a lower level property structure, with the properties determined by S_R and S_C as constituents, that is the Thought that (I seem to express) with *that everything that has the property of being red also has the property of being colored*. But this is not seem to be what follows from what Frege tells us. And, as I mentioned, the more complicated Thought seems right when we consider the cognitive significance of "Conic sections and curves of the second degree are the same property." Frege could have appealed to bifurcation: When we use "is the same as" with respect to properties, we have to existentially quantify over properties, but not otherwise. But, of course, he did not do this. It seems that he was not bothered by an aspect of his theory that bothers me.

On my interpretation of senses and Thoughts, then, they are the property structures of the *Begriffsschrift*, involving, at least, properties of objects and relations between objects; second-order properties of such properties and second-order relations between them; and third-order properties and relations such as relations being instantiated and being co-instantiated. I do not think Frege would have any objection to higher-order properties, if it turns out they are needed to get at what God or the Big Bang hath wrought.

4.4 Is There a Regress?

In an important footnote to "On Sense and Denotation," Frege tell us:

> In the case of an actual proper name such as "Aristotle" opinions as to the sense may differ. It might, for instance, be taken to be the following: the pupil of Plato and teacher of Alexander the Great. Anybody who does this will attach another sense to the sentence "Aristotle was born in Stagira" than will a man who takes as the sense of the name: the teacher of Alexander the Great who was born in Stagira. So long as the denotation remains the same, such variations of sense may be tolerated, although they are to be avoided in the theoretical structure of a demonstrative science and ought not to occur in a perfect language. ((Frege, 1960a), 58n)

We will discuss the distinction between imperfect and perfect languages below. Here the importance of the footnote is that it provides one of the very few examples of what Frege thinks the sense associated with an ordinary proper name like "Aristotle" might be. Set aside the disagreement in senses, and simply consider *the teacher of Alexander the Great who was born in Stagira*. Just how is this supposed to work? If this is the sense of "Aristotle," what Thought is expressed by "Aristotle liked syllogisms"?

Thoughts do not contain objects, so Alexander and Stagira will not be constituents of this Thought. It seems that we will have instead senses that have Alexander and Stagira as their denotations. Perhaps the sense of "Alexander the Great" is *The son of Philip II of Macedonia who conquered Persia*. But now we need three more senses to get to a Thought. This seems to threaten a regress, which is not benign if the account is to allow for knowledge of the denotation of names.

It seems that to terminate this regress, Frege needs to find modes of presentation that involve no other objects somewhere along the line. Russell eventually recognized what he called "logically proper names." Logically proper names, unlike ordinary names at the relevant stage of Russell's thinking, are not hidden descriptions but names for things with which we are directly *acquainted*. Russell thought we we were directly acquainted with our sense-data and properties and relations among those sense-data. At times he included the self on the list. Everything else we believe in and make reference to such things is based on descriptions involving such objects and properties of acquaintance. Such a doctrine does not appear in Frege. As I mentioned above, Frege is not committed to the view that the senses we grasp need to be associated with expressions. There seems to be room in his theory for senses that are directly apprehended, without other objects being involved, as the objective external properties we find in experience. This would seem to provide a strategy for avoiding regress. But Frege does not develop such a strategy. I return to the issue In Section 9.8.

4.5 Concepts and Extension

A chart of Frege's theory, considered so far, would look like this:

proper name	concept word	sentence
↓	↓	↓
sense of the proper name	sense of the concept word	sense of the sentence (Thought)
↓	↓	↓
Bedeutung of the proper name s (object)	*Bedeutung* of the concept word (concept)	*Bedeutung* of the Sentence (truth-value)

But the chart in his letter to Husserl is more complicated. There is an extra column, unlabeled, with only one entry on the denotation row, "object falling under the concept." An arrow from the entry to the left, the denotation of concept words, directs us to this column.

The extra column and the arrows reflect the integration, into the theory of sense and reference, of equipment Frege determined that he needed for his project of reducing arithmetic to logic. In the *Grundlagen*, he gives this definition of number.

> My definition is therefore as follows:
> the number which belongs to the concept F is the extension of the concept "equal to the concept F" (Section 68).

Frege became convinced, in the *Grundlagen*, that extensions had to do heavy lifting in his logical reconstruction of arithmetic. So, extensions had to have a place in the new theory of sense and denotation he developed after the *Grundlagen*. I would like to give a clear and detailed account of Frege's views about concepts and extensions in the remainder of this section, but I do not have such an account to give. The difficulties have baffled scholars and philosophers far more competent than I. They are connected with what went wrong in the *Grundgesetze*. According to the Basic Laws, for each concept f, there is an extension, the extension of f, that contains all and only objects that fall under f. That seems reasonable. But Russell asked, what about the concept of not being a member of itself? Is its extension a member of itself or not? If it is, then it falls under the concept of not being a member of itself; but then it is not.

The difficulties of interpreting Frege's views on concepts and extensions are well documented by Tyler Burge in "Frege on the Extension of Concepts, From 1884 to 1903" (Burge, 1984). Burge's article is characteristically illuminating, but even with this illumination, I have no confidence in my understanding. Still, I think I understand things well enough to see some problems, and perhaps to see in these views a motive for taking truth-values as the denotations of sentences that seems different than the argument he gives for that conclusion in "On Sense and Denotation."

Concepts are "equal" when the objects falling under them can be put in a one-to-one correlation. So, in the quote above, Frege seems to be saying, more or less, that the number five is the set of concepts that apply to exactly five things. But things are not so simple. Frege did not mean by "extension" what we mean by that word. When he wrote, what we now know as set theory was being developed by thinkers like Cantor, Dedekind, and Frege himself. *Extension* was an intuitive concept, but it was not clear exactly how it should be defined. For Frege, extensions are special case of what he calls "*Werthverlaüfe*" variously translated; I will use "courses of values." In general, functions determine courses of values, which we can think of, anachronistically, as sets of n-tuples of arguments and value(s). *Extensions* are courses of values for concepts. Still anachronistically, these are sets of n-tuples of arguments and values, where the value is either Truth or Falsity. It seems they would have to be infinitely large sets, for Frege thinks that such functions should be defined on all objects. "Caesar is taller than the number 15" is not nonsense, for example, but denotes the False.

As I said, Frege came to the conclusion that extensions had to do heavy lifting in his logicist project,[4] and his theory of sense and denotation had to find a place for them. He did not abandon properties in favor of extensions, and continued to hold, in opposition to some "extension-alist" logicians, that we only encounter extensions as the extensions *of* concepts. I appeal to authority:

> [F]or Frege predication is epistemically and logically prior to abstract objects ... the elements of a class are fixed, "delimited," only through "concepts." Elements are what fall under the concept. The relevant elements are determined, held together as a totality only through "characteristics" they have in common... ((Burge, 1984) 286)

Concepts, like all functions, are "unsaturated" entities. (I use "entity" to include both the saturated and unsaturated; Frege might disapprove.) Extensions are objects, saturated entities. Concepts are the denotations of predicates; extensions come in via the arrow in the diagram. But the only concepts eligible to be denotations are those that are extensionally individuated. A concept appearing at the level of denotation will be "the same" as any other with the same extension. (We cannot say "identical," since, for Frege, that is a relation that only holds between saturated entities.) Other concepts are consigned to the level of sense:

> A concept word stands for [bedeutet] a concept, if the word is used as is appropriate for logic ... in relation to inference, and where the laws of logic are concerned, concepts differ only insofar as their extensions are different. Now if we bear all this in mind, we shall be well able to assert "what two concept words stand for [bedeuten] is the same if and

---

[4] Russell introduced the term "logicism" in *Introduction to Mathematical Philosophy* (Russell, 1919) to describe Frege's project and his own, but apparently never used it again. It became the standard name for the view that arithmetic can be reduced to logic.

only the extensions of the corresponding concepts coincide" without being led astray by the improper use of the words "the same." And with this statement we have, I believe, made an important concession to the extensionalist logicians. They are right when they show by their preference for the extension, as against the intension, of a concept that they regard the *Bedeutung* and not the sense of the words as the essential thing for logic. The intensionalist logicians are only too happy not to go beyond the sense; for what they call the intension, if it is not an idea, is nothing other than the sense. ((Beaney, 1997), 173)

In current philosophy, the word "intension" brings to mind David Lewis's theory of intensions [1968, 1970, 1986], that they are functions from possible worlds to extensions, an idea not to be found in Frege. Lewis's theory of intensions was not offered as a definition of the term "intension." The traditional view is that:

> The *intension* of a concept consists of the qualities or properties which go to make up the concept. The extension of a concept consists of the things which fall under the concept.[5]

So the situation seems to be this. In the theory of sense and denotation ordinary properties and relations are consigned to the level of sense. Concept-words denote concepts, which are not objects, but incomplete. At least for the purposes of logic, the concepts that are denoted are extensionally individuated, unlike ordinary properties and relations. As I said, even with my shaky understanding of all the issues involved, I see problems.

4.6 Problems

4.6.1 Kerry's Problem

Frege discusses one problem, raised by Benno Kerry. Kerry objected that it is very natural to say something like "The concept horse is easily

---

[5] From Alonzo Church's entry for **Intension and extension** in Runes' *Dictionary of Philosophy* (Runes, no date).

attained," and what one says seems to be true (Kerry, 1885ff). The definite description appears to denote a concept. But on Frege's account, it cannot do so; it is the name of an object, a saturated entity, but concepts are unsaturated. But, Kerry continues, "The concept horse is not a concept" seems clearly false. Frege must take it to be true. "The concept horse is easily attained," seems true, but how can Frege account for this? Frege spends some time responding to this in "Concept and Object." He basically accepts that it is true that the concept horse is not a concept, but maintains that this is not a problem.

4.6.2 Overburdening Sense

According to Frege, "conic section" and "curve of second degree" have different senses, but denote the same concept, and so have the same extension. This seems to contrast with "creature with a heart" and "creature with a kidney." Here it seems we have different senses, and different denotations, but the same extension, at least if we set aside the accomplishments of modern medicine.

Properties that are different, but co-extensional, seem fine on the simple chart on Page 49 above, without the arrows. "Creature with a heart" and "creature with a kidney" have different senses. Intuitively they also denote different properties with the same extension. This could be made explicit by adding a new row, for extensions. But this is not the route Frege took. There seems to be no room for such properties in the new scheme.

In *The Foundations of Arithmetic*, section 68, Frege has a footnote that Tyler Burge aptly calls "remarkable" and "enigmatic" (Burge, 1984). It suggests that Frege was aware of the problem.

> I believe that for "extension of the concept" we could write simply "concept". But this would be open to the two objections:
>
> 1. that this contradicts my earlier statement that the individual numbers are objects, as is indicated by the use of the definite article in expressions like "the number two" and by the impossibility of speaking of ones, twos, etc. in the plural, as also by the fact that the

number constitutes an element in the predicate of a statement of number;

2. that concepts can have identical extension without themselves coinciding.

I am, as it happens convinced that both these objections can be met; but to do this would take us too far afield for present purposes. I assume that it is known what the extension of a concept is. ((Frege, 1950), 80n)

Whatever solution he had in mind for the first problem, he seems never to have implemented it; he does not replace "extension of the concept" with "concept" in the works after *The Foundations of Arithmetic*, which led to the difficulty Kerry raised.

The second objection seems to be the creature with a heart/creature with a kidney problem. If so, he does not ever explicitly explain his solution. But this may not have been the problem he had in mind; Burge suggests some other possible interpretations, having to do with lively debates going on at the birth of set theory.

The phrase "as is appropriate for logic. . ." suggests that Frege is thinking of perfect languages, the ones that are appropriate for logic and serious science. He is suggesting that cases in which concepts differ, but have the same extension, are irrelevant for understanding the perfect languages with which he is concerned. Or perhaps his claim is even more modest, that logicians needn't worry about them, even if professors of anatomy may have to.

But, to the extent that we want to use his theory to understand imperfect languages, the problems do not go away.

I do not claim to have given a clear view of Frege's views about concepts and extensions in this section. But, inchoate as my understanding may be, I will end on a conjecture relevant to the project of this book. Given the treatment of predicates in the theory of sense and denotation Frege had a good reason for taking truth-values to be the denotations of sentences, quite independently of the argument given for that conclusion in "On Sense and Denotation." What we have at the level of denotation are objects and extensionally individuated concepts. The latter seem to mainly serve as proxies for their extensions. Recall that extensions are (more or less, anachronistically) sequences of n-tuples of objects and truth-values. On this picture, truth-values seem a natural choice for the denotations of sentences. They are the value the function gives us with the denotations of the names as arguments. The choice also simplifies various definitions and arguments in his *Grundgesetze*.

I think it is fair to set these issues to one side, for the most part at least, when we turn to the essay that has been so influential in the philosophy of language, where they do not arise.

5

"On Sense and Denotation"

Since Frege's "On Sense and Denotation" has been required in most philosophy of language courses for well over half a century, and since most students make it through at least the first sentences of the first paragraph of required reading, most philosophers are aware of the passage with which I began this book:

> Identity gives rise to challenging questions which are not altogether easy to answer. Is it a relation? A relation between objects, or between names or signs of objects? In my *Begriffsschrift* I assumed the latter (1892) 1960a, 56.

It is somewhat unfortunate, then, that these sentences give an inaccurate statement about a philosopher's work, and in particular, the work of the very philosopher who wrote them. We are told that in the *Begriffsschrift* Frege thought that identity was a relation between names, not a relation between the objects they refer to. What a strange view! One breathes a sigh of relief that he abandoned it and went on to have more plausible ideas.

But as we have seen, Frege did not put forward this view in the *Begriffsschrift*. The concept he introduces there, *identity of content*, is a relation between "names or signs." Frege does *not* confuse that relation with identity, or hold that the latter is a relation between signs. Rather, he defines ≡, the relation between signs, *in terms of* identity, the relation between objects. In the *Begriffsschrift* names have *contents*, the objects which they refer to. The relation *identity of content* obtains between names, when the relation of identity holds between their contents. Frege's discussion may be a bit confusing, and his reasons for introducing "≡" are a bit confused, if my analysis is correct. But a confusion between identity and ≡ is simply not there. Frege's most-read words are unfair to Frege.

Frege's Detour: An Essay on Meaning, Reference, and Truth. John Perry, Oxford University Press (2019).
© John Perry DOI: 10.1093/oso/9780198812821.001.0001

5.1 Names and Descriptions

Following his exposition and criticism of his *Begriffsschrift* theory, or what he presents as his *Begriffsschrift* theory, without stopping to start a new paragraph, Frege begins the explanation of his new theory. He provides a geometrical example somewhat simpler than the one in the *Begriffsschrift*.

> Let a, b, c be the lines connecting the vertices of a triangle with the midpoints of the opposite sides. The point of intersection of a and b is then the same as the point of intersection of b and c. So we have different designations for the same point, and these names ("Point of intersection of a and b," "Point of intersection of b and c") likewise indicate the mode of presentation; and hence the statement contains true knowledge.

Here is a diagram of the sort of case Frege describes, with the common point of intersection labelled *m*.

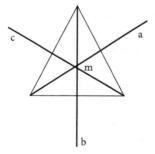

We have a function that takes two lines as arguments and a point as value: *point of intersection* $(x, y) = z$. The function has the same value for a and b as arguments, and for b and c as arguments. Frege then introduces senses:

> It is natural, now, to think of there being connected with a sign (name, combination of words, letter), besides that to which the sign refers, which may be called the denotation of the sign, also what I would like to call the sense of the sign, wherein the mode of presentation is contained. In our example, accordingly, the denotations of the expressions

"the point of intersection of a and b" and "the point of intersection of b and c" would be the same, but not their senses. The denotation of "evening star" would be the same as that of "morning star," but not their senses.

It seems that the sense of an expression has to supply necessary and sufficient conditions for being the denotation of the expression. Here as elsewhere Frege uses a definite description to explain the sense of a name. We should not conclude from this that the senses of names are "hidden descriptions." The right conclusion to draw, I think, is that Frege uses definite descriptions in explaining senses because definite descriptions do something quite plainly that senses of names need to do, but not necessarily in the same way.

5.2 Modes of Presentation and Definite Descriptions

In the quote above Frege uses the phrase "mode of presentation." (As noted, in the *Begriffsschrift* he had already spoken of "ways of determining.") He does not identify senses with modes of presentation, as many commentators do, for he says that modes of presentation are *contained* in senses. This makes sense given the meaning of "mode": a way or manner. This suggests that modes recur; we use the same modes to present one thing on one occasion, another thing on another occasion. A sense, on the other hand, is tied to one thing. So it is natural to take modes to be involved in senses, but not completely constituting them.

The term "modes of presentation" naturally suggests perception. Things are presented to us visually, via touch or taste, and so on. They can be literally presented to us, as when someone gives us a present or a menu. They can also be presented to us linguistically, by an indexical, demonstrative, name, or description. In each case we can analyse the presentation into function and arguments. A certain waiter presented me with the menu at a certain time. Another waiter, at another time, presented me with a different menu.

The descriptions in Frege's example indicate two different ways of arriving at, or determining, or one might say, being presented with, the same point m. The example is basically linguistic, but I think Frege intends for us to imagine or draw such a diagram, and follow the lines to their point of intersection. The senses of "point of intersection" are connected with objective aspects that are presented to us as various perceptual experiences. Of course, in geometry, we cannot see the points and lines we reason about, but the senses involved in our thoughts when we learn geometry are ones we acquire visually. It is not a necessary condition, for being a line, that an object be visible, but it must have properties that are also exhibited by visible objects.

One can follow a and b until they meet, or follow b and c until they meet. So, here is my suggestion for modes of presentation. They are functions in intension, that is rules for getting from some number of arguments to a single value. As such, they are properly housed at the level of sense. Different choices of arguments for the same intension can lead us to the same values, as in the example. And different modes of presentation, with suitable arguments, may also determine the same value.

So I will say, with reference to the example, that the role or function *point of intersection of* (α, β) is the *mode of presentation*. I will extend this terminology by calling the arguments, the lines a and b and c, the *presenters* and the value m, *the presented object*.

A first candidate for a sense might then be the mode of presentation, together with the presenters; the value, the presented object, is the denotation, so the mode of presentation is contained in the sense, but is not identical with it. But of course this candidate will not do. Frege is quite clear that senses do not contain objects. The senses must involve not the presenters themselves, but rather senses that determine them.

Thus the sense of "The point of intersection(a, b)" seems to be a complex, consisting of a mode of presentation and senses for the presenters, lines a and b. If we couch Frege's view in terms of conditions for a description to refer to an entity, and spell it out, we have:

"The point of intersection (a, b)" refers to y iff:

1. There is mode of presentation $M(\alpha, \beta)$, senses S, S' and lines l and l' such that
2. $M(\alpha, \beta)$ is the mode of presentation expressed by "The point of intersection of (,)"
4. S and S' are the senses of "a" and "b"
5. l and l' are the objects determined by S and S'
6. $M(l, l') = y$

This suggests something we might call "Frege's Theory of Descriptions." That phrase is a bit misleading, however. Russell wrote a famous essay, "On Denoting," that focussed on developing his theory of definite descriptions (Russell, 1905). There is no such extended discussion in Frege. But he uses many definite descriptions as examples, and had a consistent view of them.

Russell's own theory of descriptions is quite different from Frege's. Russell does not think of definite descriptions as names; he eliminates them from his basic logical language. He provides truth-conditions for the sentences that contain them, without supplying denotations, as we are using the term, for the descriptions themselves.

Consider the sentence, "The author of *Ivanhoe* found an important sceptre."[1] According to Russell, this is true if and only if there is one and only one author of *Ivanhoe*, and he found an important sceptre. On Frege's theory, the Thought the sentence expresses contains the sense of "*Ivanhoe*" and not the novel itself. The truth of the Thought requires that there is a book this sense identifies, and a unique author of that book, and that person found an important sceptre. The Thought Frege finds is not the same as the proposition Russell finds, although they would be true in the same circumstances.

In "Reference and Definite Descriptions," Keith Donnellan (Donnellan, 1966) distinguishes between *referential* and *attributive* uses of definite descriptions. Consider "The murderer of Smith is insane." Suppose that Smith was a fine fellow, who was murdered in a gruesome fashion. Looking at his body, having no idea who did the deed, one utters the sentence. This would be an attributive use; one means that whoever murdered Smith, that person was insane. But suppose later Jones has been conclusively identified as Smith's murderer, and he is convicted. In the courtroom, Jones exhibits extremely odd behavior, ranting, raving, and talking to persons who are not there. In this case, if one utters the sentence, the description would (most likely) be used referentially. One intends to say the same thing one could say with "Jones is insane."

---

[1] Sir Walter Scott and some friends rediscovered the Scottish crown jewels, which included a sceptre; it had been thought that the English had absconded with them, but Scott led a party that discovered them hidden in Edinburgh Castle.

The fact Frege groups definite descriptions with names suggests he has referential uses in mind. With our sentence, at the level of reference, we have Jones and the property of being insane, just as we would with "Jones is insane." On the other hand, the Thoughts expressed would be different, unless one's sense for "Jones" was simply *the murderer of Smith*. And the Thought expressed by "The murderer of Jones is insane" would seem to correspond to Donnellan's attributive reading.

The usual interpretation of Donnellan's distinction is that in the attributive case what one says is captured by a general proposition, basically the one Russell would assign: *A unique person murdered Smith, and that person is insane*, while in the referential case, one what one says would be a singular proposition (or a circumstance) made up of Jones and the property of being insane. It seems that the level of reference provides just the materials needed for such a circumstance; Jones is the referent of the description, and being insane the referent of the predicate. But Frege does not countenance singular propositions.

Frege seems to have an alternative treatment of definite descriptions available. It seems he could have treated definite and indefinite descriptions uniformly. That is, he could have treated "the author of *Ivanhoe*" as he treats "an author of Ivanhoe," as a concept-expression rather than a name, supplying a concept rather than an object. The definite description would provide the concept of being the unique author of the denotation of the sense of "*Ivanhoe*", which would combine with the the unsaturated predicate, to provide the saturated Thought that some object falls under both concepts, the same truth-conditions which his actual analysis provides. Thus we would have a chart (Table 5.1) with four columns:

Table 5.1 Simplified Version of Frege's Schema of Sense and Denotation, With Uniform Treatment of Descriptions

Proper Name	description	predicate	sentence
↓	↓	↓	↓
sense of the proper name	sense of the description	sense of the predicate	sense of the sentence (Thought)
↓	↓	↓	↓
denotation of the proper name (object)	[denotation of the description] (concept*→extension*)	[denotation of the concept word] (concept*→extension*)	denotation of the sentence (truth-value)

Perhaps this would have given Frege a more convincing answer to Kerry's problem. "The concept horse" *does* denote a concept after all, so the concept horse *is* a concept.

5.3 Proper Names

As mentioned, Frege's view of proper names is often assimilated to Russell's view about ordinary proper names, that they are hidden or disguised descriptions.[2] But they are certainly not disguised Russellian descriptions.

Sticking to Frege's treatment of names and descriptions, I think it is more likely that Frege held something like the opposite view, that definite descriptions are proxies for, take the place of, proper names. He calls definite descriptions "names", and as we saw gives them basically the same semantics as he gives names. In "Function and Concept," he says:

> [Consider] the expression
> "the capital of the German Empire".
> This obviously *takes the place of a proper name*, and stands for [bedeutet] an object. ... If we now split it up into the parts
> 'the capital of' and 'the German Empire', ... then [the first] part is unsaturated, where the other is complete in itself. So in accordance with what I said before, I call
>
> 'the capital of x'
>
> the expression of a function. If we take the German Empire as argument, we get Berlin as the value of the function. (p. 140 emphasis added)

Still, it is unwise to attribute to Frege either the view that names are hidden descriptions or that descriptions are proxies for names; there is insufficient evidence for either attribution. It does seem that the sense of a name has to somehow provide necessary and sufficient conditions for

---

[2] Ordinary as opposed to logically proper names, which came into Russell's theory some years after "On Denoting".

an object to be the denotation of the name, and that these conditions could be captured by a definite description. It would not follow from this that the description and the name had the same sense and that the description is a proxy for the name, or that the name is a hidden version of the description.

In fact, Frege tells us very little about the senses of proper names in "On Sense and Denotaton" — rather surprising, since so many commentators have firm opinions on the topic. Not many examples are discussed in "On Sense and Denotation." "Aristotle" occurs in the footnote on page 58, mentioned in chapter 4, in which he explains that since ordinary language is not "perfect," people may disagree about the sense of "Aristotle." "Odysseus" is mentioned as part of his argument that sentences denote to truth-values. "Kepler" comes up when he makes the point that if we incorporated the condition that "Kepler" has a denotation into the Thought that Kepler died in misery, we would need two clauses to express the negation. Only in the footnote about "Aristotle" does he give examples of the senses suitable for ordinary proper names. The alternative senses he provides to make his point are given in terms of definite descriptions:

> In the case of an actual proper name such as "Aristotle" opinions as to the sense may differ. It might, for instance, be taken to be the following: the pupil of Plato and teacher of Alexander the Great. Anybody who does this will attach another sense to the sentence "Aristotle was born in Stagira" than will a man who takes as the sense of the name: the teacher of Alexander the Great who was born in Stagira. So long as the denotation remains the same, such variations of sense may be tolerated, although they are to be avoided in the theoretical structure of a demonstrative science and ought not to occur in a perfect language. ((Frege, 1960a), 58n)

Frege does not tell us very much about how actual proper names work in imperfect languages. The importance of the footnote is often discounted, since it does not provide a paradigm case of names and senses working the way he thought they should. On the other hand, it is the only example in the 1890 Essays in which he spells out what a sense of a proper name might amount to.

There is an important point to be made about this footnote. Frege's Concept-Writing was intended to be a perfect language, and his theory of sense and denotation is intended to provide an account of perfect languages. But Frege applies the framework to imperfect languages, usually suggesting that any differences are defects that may be "tolerated" for non-scientific discourse. The evaluative implication of "perfect" does not completely square with what he said in the *Begriffsschrift*:

> I believe that I can best make the relation of my ideography to ordinary language clear if I compare it to that which the microscope has to the eye. Because of the range of its possible uses and the versatility with which it can adapt to the most diverse circumstances, the eye is far superior to the microscope. Considered as an optical instrument, to be sure, it exhibits many incompletions, which ordinarily remain unnoticed only on account of its intimate connection with our mental life. But, as soon as scientific goals demand great sharpness of resolution, the eye proves to be insufficient. The microscope, on the other hand, is perfectly suited to precisely such goals, but that is just why it is useless for all others.
>
> This ideography, likewise, is a device invented for certain scientific purposes, and one must not condemn it because it is not suited to others... ((Frege, 1967) p. 6)

This suggests a more even-handed attitude towards the difference than "perfect" and "imperfect" imply. The differences between perfect and imperfect languages are not imperfections in the latter; they may not be bugs but features related to the purposes for which language evolved, which we need to appreciate and understand if we want to understand languages that serve everyday purposes, although not the special needs of logic.

This seems especially relevant to our eventual target, indirect discourse, attitude reports, and the theory of indirect denotation. Indirect discourse and attitude reports do not occur in Concept-Writing. They have been around for a long time, in our imperfect natural languages, serving their purpose reasonably well. It would be surprising if the theory of sense and denotation did not require some supplementation to deal with imperfect languages — more than just noting how they fall short of being perfect. Understanding indirect discourse and attitude reports within a theory designed for perfect languages might be as futile as trying to understand the function of eyelids within the theory of microscopes.

5.4 Tolerable Situations

Consider the last part of Frege's footnote:

> So long as the denotation remains the same, such variations of sense may be tolerated, although they are to be avoided in the theoretical structure of a demonstrative science and ought not to occur in a perfect language (1960a, 58n).

That such variations may be tolerated, suggests the characters envisaged in the situation could carry on a conversation about Aristotle in spite of the differences in the senses they attach to the names.

Suppose Fred thinks of Aristotle in the first way, and Ethel thinks of Aristotle in the second way. It seems that if Fred says, "Aristotle liked syllogisms" he says something true, for the only person who was the student of Plato and teacher of Alexander definitely liked syllogisms. If Ethel says the same words, she says something different that is also true, that the only person who was born in Stagira and taught Alexander liked syllogisms. They express *different* true Thoughts with the same sentence, even if we assume that the senses they associate with "Plato" and "Alexander" and "Stagira" are the same.

What is it about the situation that makes it tolerable? Why do we think, in such a case, that there is a clear way in which Fred and Ethel agree? It seems that they are talking about the same person, Aristotle and predicating the same property of him, liking syllogisms. That is, they are agreeing about circumstances, not Thoughts. If this possibility is a feature of natural language, and not a bug, having circumstances in our theory might help us understand and appreciate it.

Suppose they disagree. Fred does not think anyone could actually like syllogisms, not even Aristotle, and says, "Aristotle did not like syllogisms." It seems Ethel could truthfully say, "You said that Aristotle did not like syllogisms, I say that he did like syllogisms, so we disagree about that." It seems that in conversations conducted in ordinary imperfect languages, and in reports about those conversations, something like circumstances *are* recognized. When we communicate information, the information may be expressed in different forms, involving different sentences and different Thoughts, as it gets passed from agent to agent. The circumstance gets at what is passed along; each step, the same objects and properties are involved, but not necessarily the same ways of thinking about them. And it is circumstances, not Thoughts, that get at what Fred and Ethel disagree about.

Earlier I spoke of the possibilities God might need to consider during Creation Week, and suggest they corresponded to (rather large) property structures. I will call these "God's possibilities." Human possibilities are rather different. They are what I will call "incremental." My wife and I are throwing a dinner party, with six guests and eight chairs around the table. We think its a good idea to come up with a seating plan. We take for granted we are talking about the chairs in our dining room, arranged around a table we also take for granted. And we know whom we have invited. With these objects fixed we take into account various possible constraints. Perhaps couples should not sit next to each other. We should sit near the kitchen, so we can fetch things unobtrusively, and so on. The possibilities we need to consider are not property structures, but circumstances involving particular people, particular chairs, and the relation of sitting in.

This carries over to communication. We play what I call "information games." I see a full cup of hot coffee in the kitchen at work. My mode of presentation is visual: that cup of coffee. I leave the kitchen, but continue to wonder about the hot cup of coffee. I remember the circumstance, but via a different way of thinking of the cup of coffee. It is the cup of coffee I saw a moment ago in the kitchen. I encounter Dikran, upset because he cannot find the cup of coffee he just poured for himself. I tell him, "Your cup of coffee is on the counter in the kitchen." Now I am thinking of the cup of coffee as the cup of coffee Dikran poured. Dikran goes to the kitchen and fetches his cup of hot coffee.

What happened was that I learned, visually, that a certain cup of hot coffee was on the counter in the kitchen. I had no real use for that information at that time. But then I encountered Dikran, and gave him the information, and he put it to use. One person picked up information at one time, and then, via a causal interaction, another person was able to put the information to use in guiding his actions. Perhaps Thoughts are the right thing to use to deal with the truth-conditions and cognitive significance of what I learned in the kitchen and might have expressed by saying to no one in particular "That is a cup of hot coffee." And perhaps they are the right thing for understanding the truth-conditions of the cognitive state Dikran went into as a result of our conversation. But they are not very good at getting at the information I remembered and communicated and he put to use. I did not care whether Dikran thought of the cup via the same mode of presentation I had, and he did not worry about it either. What was crucial was that it was the same cup, that the cup I remembered and told him about was the same one he poured for himself. What was crucial was the circumstance. Circumstances might have some useful purpose in our semantics, even if they only get at what we might call the incremental conditions of truth, and do not exhaust the cognitive significance of the beliefs we have about the objects in the circumstances.

So back to Fred and Ethel. Why is the difference in the Thoughts they have, as they discuss Aristotle, tolerable? Clearly because they have established that they are agreeing and disagreeing about circumstances involving the same fellow. We have all sorts of institutions for dealing with information, from names in our ordinary imperfect languages to libraries and social security numbers, to help give people confidence that they are conversing about the same objects, however different their modes of presentation of those objects might be.

"Says that," and the attitude verbs generally, are a part of ordinary, imperfect language. They were there before Aristotle invented logic and came to enjoy syllogisms, and no doubt before written languages were invented. It seems very unlikely that the rules implicit in using these constructions incorporate constraints appropriate to Frege's perfect languages. This strongly suggests that Frege's theory of indirect denotation is not directly applicable to ordinary language, the natural home of these constructions.

As we shall see in Section 5.5, Frege gives us a theory of attitude verbs that works, at most, for perfect languages used to discuss God's possibilities. Applied to imperfect languages, Ethel's report of what Fred said comes out false, which seems wrong. As the reader may have guessed, I will return to this theme.

5.5 Sentences and Truth-Values

Having discussed names, one might expect that Frege would next discuss the sense and denotation of concept words. But he had already told us that he will not:

> It is clear from the context that by "sign" and "name" I have here understood any designation representing a proper name, whose referent is thus a definite object (this word taken in the widest range), but no concept and no relation, which shall be discussed further in another article. (210)

Indeed, there is nothing in the essay to inform a reader that ordinary intensional properties are not the denotations of predicates. Above I conjectured that Frege's treatment of concepts and extensions made the choice of truth-values as the denotations of sentences inevitable. Whatever the merits of that conjecture, these reasons do not appear in "On Sense and Denotation."

After discussing the confusions of skeptics and idealists, he turns to sentences and Thoughts. This discussion ends with the choice of truth-values as the denotations of sentences, and that leads to the doctrine of indirect denotation, and, according to me, Frege's Detour.

The picture we might have of Frege's theory at this point in the essay, if we had studied the *Begriffsshrift* and now were being introduced to his new theory, is something like the diagram below. We would have to fill in the column for concept words ourselves, as indicated by italics, by analogy with what he has told us about names.

proper name	*concept word*	sentence
↓	↓	↓
sense of the proper name	*sense of the concept word*	sense of the sentence (Thought)
↓	↓	↓
Bedeutung of the proper name s (object)	*Bedeutung of the concept word* (concept)	*Bedeutung* of the Sentence (???)

One might then expect that the lower right hand cell will be filled so that the we have a commutative diagram. We can get to the bottom right cell in two ways, which should give the same result. We can start on the second row, going to the right and then down. Or can come down the columns on the left, and go across the bottom row. Across the top we have a function that takes us from a pair of senses of the expressions to a Thought expressed by the sentence. Going down we have a function from Thoughts to the denotations they determine, with the world as a parameter. Going down in the left two columns, we have a function that gives us a the pair of denotations determined by the same pair of senses, with help from the world. Then, moving to the right, we have a function takes us from this pair of denotations to the denotation of the sentence.

At this point, it might occur to us that there are two candidates for the lower right cell. They might be circumstances, both first order and higher order, that instantiate the Thought, given the denotations of the sub-sentential expressions. Or they might be truth-values. And it might seem to us that circumstances make a bit more sense. First, it sounded at the beginning of the essay as if Frege was adding the level of *Sinne* (Senses) to the theory to supplement *Bedeutungen*, so why should they not be just what they were in the *Begriffsschrift*? Second, if Frege chooses circumstances, then the world can come into things in a limited way, along both routes, as seem appropriate for semantics. Coming down in the left columns, the world helps to determine the denotations of the relevant senses. Coming down in the right column, the same facts will determine which circumstances instantiate the Thought. The diagram as a whole would show give us, by two routes, the information a competent speaker, who knows what the expressions denote, grasps. This seems like an appropriate thing for a semantical theory to provide. Such a speaker would then need to acquire more information about the world to determine the truth-value.

Consider once again:

(10) Hesperus is moonless.

(11) Phosphorus is moonless.

The diagrams for these two sentences would exhibit their important difference in cognitive significance, in the upper right cell, for Thoughts. But it would also exhibit an important way in which they are the same, in the lower right cell. Two Babylonians, staring at the moon, utter (10) and (11). We get:

Name	Concept Word	Sentence
Hesperus	is moonless	Hesperus is moonless
↓	↓	↓
Being the unique evening planet	the property of not having one of *those*	The Thought that the evening planet does not have one of *those*
↓	↓	↓
The planet Venus	the property of being moonless	The circumstance: Being moonless, the planet Venus

Name	Concept Word	Sentence
Phosphorus	is moonless	Phosphorus is moonless
↓	↓	↓
Being the unique morning planet	the property of not having one of *those*	The Thought that the morning planet does not have one of *those*
↓	↓	↓
The planet Venus	the property of being moonless	The circumstance: Being moonless, the planet Venus

We can accept Frege's insight that circumstances do not capture cognitive significance. But it does not follow that they do not get at something important. It is important that "Tully was an orator" and "Cicero was an orator" do not have the same cognitive significance. But it is also important that, in spite of that, they stand for the same circumstance. Circumstances get at something important that sentences can have in common even when they have different cognitive significance. This is highlighted in the bottom right cell. It seems like this might be useful in understanding imperfect languages, where things are tolerable if participants in a conversation can deal with different names with different senses, and even different senses for the same name, so long as they are sure that they are dealing with the same circumstance.

But this is not the choice Frege makes.

5.6 The Senses and Denotations of Sentences

Frege begins by explaining Thoughts:

> We now inquire concerning the sense and denotation of an entire
> declarative sentence. Such a sentence contains a Thought. Is this
> Thought, now, to be regarded as its sense or its denotation? Let us
> assume for the time being that the sentence has a denotation! If we
> now replace one word of the sentence by another having the same
> denotation, but a different sense, this can have no influence upon the
> denotation of the sentence.
>
> Yet we can see that in such a case the Thought changes; since, e.g.,
> the Thought expressed by the sentence "the morning star is a body
> illuminated by the sun" differs from that expressed by "the evening star
> is a body illuminated by the sun." Anybody who did not know that the
> evening star is the morning star might hold the one thought to be true,
> the other false. The thought, accordingly, cannot be the denotation of
> the sentence, but must rather be considered as the sense.
>
> ((Frege, 1960a), p. 62)

In footnote 5, Frege reminds us that by "Thought" (*Gedanke*) he does
not mean something subjective; they do not consist of mental states or
brain perturbations. They are also objective rather than subjective in the
sense that the who is doing the speaking, thinking or in general *grasping*
of the Thought, and when and where they are when grasping it, does not
change its conditions of truth. Different subjects may associate different
Thoughts with the same sentence, but that is a different matter. Once
we have the Thought, we have the truth-conditions. According to Frege
in "The Thought," Thoughts are denizens of a Third Realm of abstract
objects, that, unlike thoughts in the subjective sense, can be grasped by
different people.

So Thoughts are the senses of sentences. What are their denotations?
Frege first asks whether sentences *must* have a denotation. It is here that
"Odysseus" comes up. You are reading Homer's poem and come across
the sentence "Odysseus was set ashore at Ithaca while sound asleep." If
you are reading for aesthetic pleasure it suffices that the name and the
sentence have senses. You read, you imagine, you enjoy the epic. But if

you are reading to learn about what happened after the Trojan War, you will be interested not only in the aesthetic properties of the sentence; you will be assuming that it has a further property of being true or being false. When you find out that *The Odyssey* is fiction, and "Odysseus" does not denote anyone, you will quit worrying about whether the sentence is true or false.

On Frege's scheme, the sense of a complex expression is determined by the senses of its parts, and the denotation of such an expression is determined by the denotations of its parts. Something will be missing with a sentence that has a part with no denotation. It will not have a truth-value. Nothing is missing at the level of sense; the sentence has a sense so long as its parts have senses. Thus a sentence having a truth-value must be an issue of denotation, not of sense. He ends this long paragraph by saying:

> It is the striving for truth that drives us always to advance from the sense to the denotation. ((Frege, 1960a) p. 63)

He sums up his argument so far in the next short paragraph:

> We have seen that the denotation of a sentence may always be sought, whenever the denotations of its components are involved; and that this is the case when and only when we are inquiring after the truth value. ((Frege, 1960a) p. 63)

He then states his conclusion at the beginning of the next paragraph, another long one:

> We are therefore driven into accepting the truth value of a sentence as its denotation. By the truth value of a sentence I understand the circumstance that it is true or false.[3] ((Frege, 1960a) p. 63)

---

[3] We see a brief re-emergence of circumstances in the last sentence. If we take this literally, it would seem to be quite important. It would suggest that circumstances do not really disappear from Frege's theory. But I do not think that "circumstance" is the key word in this passage. Perhaps "sentence" is. I think Frege is simply reminding us that, in spite of Thoughts and their importance, it is ultimately sentences that denote Truth or Falsity. Sentences express Thoughts. Thoughts and other senses *determine* denotations. But, ultimately, it is the words that do the denoting, not their senses, and in particular it is sentences that denote truth-values. Thoughts, along with what actually happens in the world, *determine* the truth-values; sentences denote them.

It is the move from the summary to the statement of the conclusion that is crucial. Let's grant Frege that we look for the denotation of a sentence only when we are confident that its components have denotations. Why does this *drive* us to take the truth-value of the sentence as its denotation? If a name has a sense but no denotation, we will not have the object we need to arrive at a circumstance. Indeed, one might think this is the explanation for there being no truth-value.

So, it seems to me, circumstances are the natural choice for the denotations of sentences, and Frege gives us no good reason for choosing truth-values instead. But perhaps he had more against circumstances than that they do not capture cognitive significance. Perhaps they really just will not work; perhaps they do not even quite make sense. Alonzo Church found the seeds of an argument to this effect in "On Sense and Denotation," which is now usually called "the slingshot."

In the next chapter, I shift gears, beginning to develop my own view about the issues Frege grappled with. I begin by arguing that Frege's *Begriffsschrift* had the resources to deal with the identity problems, if he abandons the principle of unique content, by using ideas from what I call the "reflexive-referential" theory. Then, in the following chapter, I will return to circumstances and use these to argue that Church's slingshot does not work.

6

Solving the Identity Problems

I think Frege's Basic Theory in the *Begriffsschrift* has the resources to solve the problems at the end of Chapter 3. I think he had the beginnings of this strategy in his concept of "bifurcation," — often considered the most unpromising part of his Section 8 solution. But he was not in a position to develop it, because of his adherence to the doctrine of unique semantic content, principle (A) in my list of false doctrines along the detour. Once we have this solution in hand, we can also disarm the slingshot.

6.1 A Common Sense Solution

A brief review. Consider:

(4) Hesperus = Hesperus

(5) Hesperus = Phosphorus

(6) "Hesperus" and "Phosphorus" refer to the same thing.

(7) The first planet to appear in the evening sky is the last planet to disappear from the morning sky.

(10) Hesperus is moonless.

(11) Phosphorus is moonless.

If sentences refer to circumstances, then, since (5) is true, (4) and (5) refer to the same circumstance. But we can learn (6) from (5) but not from (4). That is the name problem. And if we were taught "Hesperus" and "Phosphorus" in the way my Babylonians were, we can learn (7) from (5) but not from (4). That is the co-instantiation problem. Finally, one can agree with (10) but disagree or be very dubious about (11), even though

Frege's Detour: An Essay on Meaning, Reference, and Truth. John Perry, Oxford University Press (2019).
© John Perry DOI: 10.1093/oso/9780198812821.001.0001

they refer to the same circumstance. That is the general problem. It seems if we can take care of these, we can handle Wilson's problem.

To explain my point of view, I will start with the general problem, (10) and (11), with no identity sign to mislead us.

Suppose, unlike my Babylonians, but like most contemporary philosophers, you often do not remember whether Hesperus is "the morning one or the evening one." You are going to lecture on Frege, and want to make sure you have it straight. You find a helpful *Wikipedia* entry. You find out that Hesperus is indeed the evening one. You also encounter (10).

(10)   Hesperus is moonless.[1]

Would you, or at least could you, learn from (10) not only that Venus is moonless, the circumstance that is the conceptual content of (10) in the *Begriffsschrift* framework, but also that "Hesperus" is the name of a planet with no moons? It seems quite obvious that you could. Perhaps someone looking over your shoulder sees the name "Hesperus" and asks, "To what does the name 'Hesperus' refer"? Surely you would be in a position to say, " 'Hesperus' is the name of a moonless planet."

Frege thought that by introducing "≡", he introduced a bifurcation in the meanings of all names. Sometimes they stand for their references, other times they stand for themselves. But something like this bifurcation was already there, independently of the introduction of "≡".

In general, by using expressions to convey information about things, we also convey information about the expressions. This is due to the truth-conditions of the sentences containing the expressions. This is one thing that makes language learning possible. If I point to Fred and say, "This man is Fred," and you assume I know what I am talking about, you will learn that the man's name is "Fred," for otherwise I would have said something false. Once you know the name, I can use it to tell you about Fred. But I can also use Fred, by pointing to him as I use the name, to teach you the name.

You can also use falsehoods to teach the meanings of expressions; it is the truth-conditions, not the truth-value, that is important. I put a platter full of an ugly green vegetable on the table in front of my grandchildren

---

[1] As far as I know, this sentence does not actually occur in a *Wikipedia* entry.

saying, "You will enjoy the kale." They will learn that the vegetable I have served them is called "kale," even if they suspect I am lying. If it were not called "kale," my statement would not make much sense. The fact that "kale" names this wretched (but healthy) vegetable is one of the truth-conditions of my remark, which they will soon find to have been false.

These cases show that the doctrine of unique content is incorrect. The sentence "Hesperus is moonless" as used by our Babylonians, is true only if *Venus is moonless*. And it is true only if *"Hesperus" refers to something with no moons*. These are both truth-conditions for the Sentence, and they are different.

Now back to:

(10) Hesperus is moonless.

According to the *Begriffsschrift* theory with Section 8 set aside, under what conditions is (10) true? The following seems correct:

(a) There is an x, such that "Hesperus" refers to x, and x is moonless.

If we add that, in fact, "Hesperus" refers to Venus, then we can give the truth-conditions as:

(b) Venus is moonless.

Here we have two different statements of the truth-conditions of (10). They are not inconsistent; (b) specifies *one way* (10) might meet the truth-conditions given in (a), and, in fact, might be the only way it can do so, given that "Hesperus" refers to Venus.

Condition (a) is on "Hesperus": that it names a planet with no moons. If the name "Hesperus" meets that condition, (10) is true. Condition (b) is on the planet Venus, the object to which "Hesperus" refers". Venus could meet this condition, even if the word "Hesperus" had never been assigned to it; indeed, it met this condition long before there was life or language on earth. But given these things, by meeting condition (b), Venus *completes* a set of conditions sufficient for (10) to be true.

Condition (b) gives us the *incremental* truth-conditions of the sentences, *given* (a), and the fact that "Hesperus" names Venus.

This last point can seem a bit puzzling: (b) is supposed to give the truth-conditions for (10), a sentence. But (b) puts no condition on (10) or any other sentence; it put conditions on the planet Venus. The puzzle disappears when we see that (b) is only telling us *what else* is necessary for the truth of (10) *given* (a) and, in addition, the fact "Hesperus" refers to Venus.

What happened when you read (10) in the *Wikipedia* article? Simply this. When we say that a sentence is true we mean that its truth-conditions are satisfied. When we read or hear a sentence, and accept it as true, we accept that its truth-conditions are satisfied. Usually, we think of those conditions as conditions on the objects and concepts referred to. We start by hearing or seeing expressions, and immediately go from the expressions to the objects and properties to which they refer. What are the truth-conditions of (10)? It is natural to say that Venus is moonless; that is, that Venus has the property of being moonless. That is the condition the entities referred to by the two expressions have to meet, for (10) to be true.

But Venus's being moonless is *not* sufficient by itself for (10) to be true. Venus had no moons long before Babylonian and English were invented, much less the *Wikipedia*. Venus having no moons *specifies* the truth-conditions for (10), *given* what is given — the language is English, "having no moons" refers to the property of having no moons, and "Hesperus" refers to Venus. Given that, (10) is true if the reference of "Hesperus" has no moons, that is, if Venus is moonless.

We do not always go directly to the objects and properties referred to. If you use a word I do not understand, I may ask you what it means, or look it up in the dictionary. You say, "Murdoch's *Under the Net* is picaresque." I have read the novel, but still have no idea whether what you said is true or false. I do know that if what you said is true, "picaresque" stand for a property that Murdoch's novel possesses. I know the truth-conditions of your utterance, but I do not know them in a way that allows me to decide whether it is true of false.

Am I claiming that *what we say*, when we utter (10), is something about names? That (10) really does have a name as part of its subject matter? That it really refers to the circumstance of "Hesperus" being a name of the second planet from the sun, rather than the circumstance of Venus being the second planet from the sun?

None of the above. I am claiming that we should not simply identify *the* truth-conditions of a sentence with the conditions its truth puts on the things the expressions in the sentence refer to. Doing so is the source of the doctrine of unique content. These are *usually* the crucial conditions; they *usually* comprise the information we want to convey. They are what we would normally reckon as *what is said* or *the proposition expressed*. The practice of conveying information about the objects to which we refer is central to language; we cannot understand how it evolved, or how it is used, without appreciating that. But, for all that, the conditions on the objects referred to by the expressions in a sentence do *not* exhaust the truth-conditions of the sentence. Other truth-conditions can be conveyed, and are often what we are trying to convey. That is, the doctrine of unique content is wrong.

If this were not so, teaching language would be baffling. A Babylonian parent points to Venus and says, "That is Hesperus." The child learns a name of the planet. Perhaps the parent is secretly supplying quotation marks? Is she is really saying, "We call that 'Hesperus' "? Does she have to start the child's language learning by explaining quotation marks? Surely not. She manages to convey, by saying "That is Hesperus," what could be conveyed with "We call that 'Hesperus.'" But now we have the mystery step. How does she manage to convey information about a word, with a sentence about a planet? She can do so, because the child understands at least inchoately the truth-conditions of sentences of the form "That is N" and realizes that the parent is pointing at a certain object in the heavens, and so the sentence can be true only if "Hesperus" is a name of that object.

What is special about identity sentences is not that they mysteriously convey information about the expressions in them, because of some ad-hoc mechanism of bifurcation. It is rather that to a degree not matched by other sentences, conveying such information is often, almost always, the point of uttering them. The parent tells the child "That is Hesperus" to teach the child the name "Hesperus." I say, "San Sebastian is Donostia" not to inform you of the circumstance of San Sebastian being self-identical, but to inform you that "Donostia" is a name of San Sebastian, or the other way around. No mechanism special to identity sentences that transports us from "=" to "≡" is involved. We all know, as inchoately as a child or as explicitly as a logician, how language works, and that a sentence of the form "*aRb*" is true if "*R*" stands for a relation that the objects named by "*a*" and "*b*" stand in. For "San Sebastian is Donostia" to be true, the name "Donostia" *must* stand for San Sebastian.

6.2 Three Kinds of Truth-Conditions

Now, with these ideas in mind, I want to look more closely and systematically at the truth-conditions Frege's *Begriffsschrift* theory, without relying on Section 8, provide for the key sentences in the identity problems. However, so as not to become totally obsessed with planets, I will start with a couple of my favorite philosophers.[2] Consider:

(12)   Bratman is taller than Lawlor.

This sentence is true iff:

> There are objects x and y and a relation ψ such that:
> (a) ψ is the relation to which "is taller than" refers;
> (b) x is the object to which "Bratman" refers;
> (c) y is the object to which "Lawlor" refers;
> (d)   The circumstance that x has ψ to y is a fact.

These truth-conditions are not what we would ordinarily think of as the truth-conditions for our sentence. They are not conditions on Bratman, Lawlor, or the relation of being taller than. But, in fact, they provide necessary and sufficient conditions for the truth of (12), simply not the ones that naturally come to mind. These are conditions on the expressions in sentence (12) *itself*. So, I call them *reflexive* truth-conditions. "Reflexive" is not meant to convey anything metaphysically deep. I will borrow a term from Heidegger later; here I am borrowing from Reichenbach (Reichenbach, 1947). Nor is it meant to imply that the sentence (12) contains a reference to itself. It simply means what the

---

[2] The ideas developed in this section were first explained in (Israel and Perry, 1990). They are more fully explained in (Perry, 2012a) and (Korta and Perry, 2011).

reflexive pronoun conveys, that these are conditions on the sentence (12) *itself.*

Note that even this is not quite right. I have already engaged in a bit of role-identification. The tag "(12)" names a sentence. What follows the right parenthesis shows us which words make it up, and what grammatical structure it has. If I had ambitions of saying something interesting about grammar, I would have supplied a couple of subscripts for the noun phrases and the verb phrase, or a linguist's tree, to make the information about (12) explicit. What I have called the "reflexive" truth-conditions take the expressions and the grammatical structure of (12) as *given,* and give us what *else* has to be the case for (12) to be true.

Given the reflexive truth-conditions, and *in addition* the facts that "is taller than" refers to the relation of being taller than, and that "Bratman" refers to Michael Bratman, and that "Lawlor" refers to Krista Lawlor, what *else* has to be the case for (12) to be true? Given these facts about reference, (12) is true if and only if the circumstance that Michael Bratman is taller than Krista Lawlor is a fact, that is, if and only if Michael Bratman is taller than Krista Lawlor.

I call these the *referential* truth-conditions of (12). So we have two sets of truth-conditions for the same sentence. They are not the same, but they are consistent. In general, if we specify the conditions for an object to have some property by quantifying over objects that play certain roles relative to that object, we obtain more specific conditions for that object to have that property when we identify those objects.

I tell you, "There is an exam coming up. Elwood will pass the course if and only if Elwood passes that exam." If I am right, and the exam coming up is in fact the final, Elwood will pass the course if and only if he passes the final. We have two sets of necessary and sufficient conditions. They are consistent. The latter is *specification* of the former; that is, the specific manner in which that set of conditions has to be fulfilled, given the fact that the upcoming exam is the final.

The reflexive truth-conditions for (12) quantify over the objects that are referred to by the expressions in (12). When we fill in these occupants of the roles, that is, specify the objects so referred to, we end up with a condition on those objects: that Bratman is taller than Lawlor, that is, the referential truth-conditions. The referential truth-conditions of a sentence are one way the sentence could satisfy its reflexive truth-conditions, and the only way it can if our identifications of the referents are correct.

Let us return to our problems. First, let us consider the reflexive and referential conditions of (5) on the Basic Theory, treating it like any other sentence of the form "*aRb*" is treated in the *Begriffsschrift*. First the reflexive truth-conditions:

> There are objects *x* and *y* and a relation ψ such that:
> (a)   *x* is the object to which "Hesperus" refers;
> (b)   *y* is the object to which "Phosphorus" refers;
> (c) ψ is the binary relation to which "=" refers;
> (d)   The circumstance that *x* has ψ to *y* is a fact.

The referential truth-conditions will simply be that Venus is identical with Venus. Hence, the referential truth-conditions will be the same for:

(4)   Hesperus = Hesperus

and that is the problem.

The reflexive truth-conditions for (4) and (5), however, are different. The reflexive truth-conditions for (5) put conditions on both names. The reflexive truth-conditions for (4) put conditions only on "Hesperus."

This does not yet provide a direct solution for our problem. However, we can also recognize additional levels of truth-conditions, *hybrid* levels, where only some of the objects that play the relevant roles are identified.

If we start with the reflexive truth-conditions of (5), and then identify the reference of "=" as identity, but leave the references of "Hesperus" or "Phosphorus" unidentified, here is what *else* has to be the case for (5) to be true:

> There are objects *x* and *y* such that:
> (a)   *x* is the object to which "Hesperus" refers;
> (b)   *y* is the object to which "Phosphorus" refers;
> (c)   The circumstance that *x* is identical with *y* is a fact.

And for (4):

> There are objects x and y such that:
> (a) x is the object to which "Hesperus" refers;
> (b) y is the object to which "Hesperus" refers;
> (c)   The circumstance that $x = y$ is a fact.

These hybrid truth-conditions give us what we need. They give us exactly what Frege introduced "$\equiv$" to provide, but do so without Section 8 and the new symbol. The difference between (4) and (5) does not involve a mystery step. It simply involves recognition of the fact that sentences may have the same referential truth-conditions, but differ in their reflexive and hybrid truth-conditions and, in virtue of that difference, can be used to convey different bits of information. Sentence (5) is true if and only if 'Hesperus" and 'Phosphorus" co-refer, a non-trivial fact, that one might learn from an utterance of (5), and which might be an important step in gaining important astronomical knowledge. But (4) only puts conditions on 'Hesperus" and conveys no such non-trivial knowledge.

This solution extends to the fourth problem. Sentences (10) and (11) have different hybrid truth-conditions. If we take it as given that "is moonless" refers to the property of having no moons:

(10)   is true iff "Hesperus" refers to an object that is moonless.

(11)   is true iff "Phosphorus" refers to an object that is moonless.

Thus, someone who knows (10) could learn something from (11), and vice-versa.

It also extends to Wilson's problem. The difference in cognitive significance between "Hesperus is the same size as Hesperus" and "Hesperus is the same size as Phosphorus" emerges at the level of hybrid contents. For the second sentence to be true "Phosphorus" must refer to a planet that is the same size as the one "Hesperus" refers to, but this is not a hybrid condition of truth for the first.

6.3 Wider Applications

This sort of back and forth in our semantic thinking that is exhibited by my suggested solution to Frege's problems is quite apparent with a number of other phenomena that perhaps would not arise in perfect languages, but are common in imperfect ones. Ambiguity is one example. You say, "I'm going to the bank to catch some fish." I'm puzzled. You cannot catch fish at a bank. Then I realize that you mean *riverbank*; that is the meaning of "bank" that makes sense of your remark, giving it truth-conditions that might be satisfied. When a person uses a racial or ethnic slur there is often an acceptable term with the same extension, or at least the same intended extension. But the message conveyed when the acceptable term replaces the slur will not convey the same message. Richard Vallée explores this phenomena in "Slurring and common knowledge of ordinary language" (Vallée, 2014). This paper is included in his book *Words and Contents* along with other valuable papers in which he applies the "pluri-propositionalist" framework to color predicates, comparison classes, and various sorts of ambiguity as well as some traditional but difficult philosophy of languages issues, such as "we".

Joana Garmendia employs the framework in her neo-Gricean account of irony (Garmendia, 2015).

Maria de Ponte uses it to discuss temporal indexicals in relation to speech acts in "Promises, the present, and 'now'" (de Ponte, 2017a) , and she and Kepa Korta take a new look at an old root canal in (de Ponte and Korta, 2017).

Eros Corazza has applied the framework to implicatures, illocutionary acts, Quine's sentence "Giorgione was so-called because of his size" and a number of other issues in semantics and pragmatics (Corazza, 2010, 2011a,b). And his forthcoming book *Proper Names* uses the framework to provide what will become the definitive account these pesky creatures. Corazza and Korta use the framework to discuss alternative approaches to semantics in "Minimalism, Contextualism, and Contentualism" (Corazza and Korta, 2010).

Chris Genovesi uses the framework to discuss both theoretical and empirical issues in figurative language in his groundbreaking dissertation, *Food for Thought: Metaphor in Language and Cognition* (Genovesi, 2019).

And Leonard Clapp and Armando Lavalle use the framework in their treatment of a problem about identity statements that I will not discuss, although it has become a central issue at the intersection of loigic, metaphyics, epistemology, and the philosophy of language in

"Multipropositionalism and Necessary A Posteriori Identity Statements" (Clapp and Lavalle, forthcoming).

6.4 Two Solutions?

I would like to end this chapter by comparing the *Begriffsschrift*-based solution I have given to the Name Problem to the one Frege provides in "On Sense and Denotation." But another annoying problem arises. He does not provide one.[3]

In the first paragraph of the essay, having given an inaccurate statement of his *Begriffsschrift* view, Frege seems to explain his own solution to the second problem. Adapted to my fable, it is the sentence "Hesperus = Phosphorus" *itself*, not some other sentence involving "≡" that carries, for semantically competent Babylonians, the information that the property of being the first planet to appear in the evening and the property of being the last planet to disappear in the morning are co-instantiated. The "ways of determination" of the *Begriffsschrift* have become senses. They are part of the content, the Thought expressed. The sentence "Hesperus = Phosphorus" does not express the circumstance that Venus is Venus, but rather expresses the Thought that one thing is both the first planet to appear in the evening and the last planet to disappear in the morning. If we understand the identity sentence (5), we grasp this thought.

But, on this account, what is the solution to the Name Problem? That is, how can one learn that "Hesperus" and "Phosphorus" co-refer from "Hesperus = Phosphorus"? The Thought that one planet is both the first star to appear in the evening and the last to disappear in the morning contains no information about the names "Hesperus" and "Phosphorus."

Frege goes on to deny that first problem, the difference in what we can learn about *names* from (5) and (4), is a problem after all.

> If the sign "a" is distinguished from the sign "b" only as object (here, by means of its shape), not as a sign (i.e., not by the manner in which it designates), *the cognitive value of a = a becomes essentially equal to that of a=b, provided a=b is true.* [emphasis added]

---

[3] See also (Corazza and Korta, 2015) and (de Ponte, Korta, and Perry, Forthcomingb).

One might think he is thinking about the case in which "a" and "b" are just marks, not yet assigned as names to anything. But then it would make no sense to say, "provided a = b is true."

As I understand this, Frege means that if we consider "Hesperus = Phosphorus," and put aside the senses of the names, its cognitive value is —"essentially"— no different from "Hesperus = Hesperus." There is something right about this. If we do not know the senses, we cannot glean any *astronomical* information from either sentence, even though we recognize the former is synthetic. In effect Frege is ruling about knowledge of co-denotation of names as being of any cognitive value, or at least of any "essential" cognitive value. In the *Begriffsschrift* Frege recognizes that we somehow get from "A = B" to "A ≡ B", but does not explain how. In the "On Sense and Denotation," he does not explain how, but simply denies there is a problem.

Edwina shows that this cannot be right. Edwina hears the new discovery, "Hesperus = Phosphorus," before her parents have taken her out in the evening and morning and taught her the ways of determination associated with these words. She learns from this that "Hesperus" and "Phosphorus," which she has not previously encountered, are names. But for all she knows, "Hesperus" and "Phosphorus" could be names of pet birds, or children, or streets. She does not learn anything about astronomy. But then Edwina learns that the way of determination associated with "Hesperus" is being the first planet to appear in the evening, and that the way of determination associated with "Phosphorus" is being the last planet to disappear in the morning. From this, together with what she *already* learned from "Hesperus = Phosphorus," Edwina learns a substantial astronomical fact, that the first planet to appear in the evening is the last star to disappear in the morning. She would not have learned this if her staring point had been "Hesperus = Hesperus." The information about names Edwina learns from (5) may not be very interesting in and of itself. But (5) does *not* have the same cognitive significance as (4), by the inference criterion.

We can account for what Edwina learns on the theory of sense and denotation. We need a Thought that is about names, that we learn from (5). This requires senses *for* the names themselves, in addition to the senses for other things with which the names are associated. Expressions are naturally individuated by spelling, although of course, more complicated theories can be found. Assuming this simple theory, the sense of "Hesperus" will be *the expression consisting of an "H" followed by an "e"*, etc. and similarly for "Phosphorus". Call the relevant senses S_H and S_P. The Thought that Edwina grasps is that there is are names that are the denotation of S_H and S_P and an object that is the denotation of both names; call this Thought *HP*. *HP* seems like a perfectly respectable Thought. This account would seem adequate for perfect languages, and extendable with some complications to imperfect ones. Perhaps Frege thought it was too obvious to need explanation. But in that case his remarks in the paragraph quoted above are hard to explain.

I think the explanation for this omission is that the Thought attributed to Edwina on this account would not fit well with the doctrine of unique content. This thought is not the Thought expressed by "Hesperus = Phosphorus." That Thought will involve the senses *of* "Hesperus" and "Phosphorus," not S_H and S_P, the senses *for* those names, that is, the senses that determine those names as denotation.

If we adapt the reflexive-referential view to the theory of sense and denotation, things work out fine. Remember that among other things Edwina learns that "Hesperus" and "Phosphorus" are names when she hears "Hesperus = Phosphorus." To account for this bit of information we need to start with a more basic level for reflexive content. Only the grammar of the sentence and the sense and denotation of "=" are given. Given that, for the sentence to be true, S_H and S_P have to be senses that determine names as their referents, those names have to denote, and they have to denote the same thing, whether that thing is a planet or a street in Baghdad. This is a condition on senses, not names or planets.

It will not be too hard for Edwina to figure out that the names in question are "Hesperus" and "Phosphorus." and so to move to the first hybrid truth-conditions: The sentence is true if and only if "Hesperus" and "Phosphorus" denote the same thing. Then, when her parents take her out in the evening and morning, and she associates the proper senses with those names, she will learn that for the sentence to be true, the first planet to appear in the night sky is also the last to disappear from the morning sky.

Frege returns to the issue of identity in the closing paragraph of "On Sense and Denotation":

Let us return to our starting point!

If we found "a = a" and "a = b" to have different cognitive values, the explanation is that for the purpose of knowledge, the sense of the sentence, viz., the thought expressed by it, is no less relevant than its denotation, i.e., its truth value. If now a = b, then indeed the denotation of "b" is the same as that of "a," and hence the truth value of "a = b" is the same as that of "a = a." In spite of this, the sense of "b" may differ from that of "a," and thereby the sense expressed in "a = b" differs from that of "a = a." In that case the two sentences do not have the same cognitive value. If we understand by "judgment" the advance from the thought to its truth value, as in the above paper, we can also say that the judgments are different.

Discussion of the problem that led Frege, 15 years earlier, to retiring "=" and come up with Section 8 , is here treated with the word "indeed." It does seem to have become an unimportant problem for him.

The structure of his theory seems to shield us from the problem. Names are objects, and so not constituents of Thoughts. So the name problem will not arise in the Realm of Thought. We have properties in Thoughts, but relation of identity does not hold between properties. How could the problem arise?

However, the problem may arise. Thoughts are objects; on the theory of indirect reference they are denoted by that-clauses. Can we grasp the same Thought, twice over, without realizing it? This is related to the problems Horty discusses in *Frege on Definitions* (2007). It seems that we might have one complicated formulation of a Thought, and another formulation of the same Thought, using defined terms, that is much more easily grasped. There seems to be a difference in cognitive significance of some sort. It would seem that this cannot be accounted for by their expressing different Thoughts, for if the definitions are sound, they should express the same Thought. Horty plausibly thinks that Frege needs to bring in something like what I call "episodes" below, to justify his view of the utility of definitions.

7

Disarming the Slingshot

But perhaps my pleas for circumstances should fall on deaf ears. Perhaps there is just something wrong with circumstances that makes them ineligible to be the denotations of sentences. As mentioned above, (Alonzo Church 1943, 1956) found at least the seeds of an argument to this effect in Frege's essay. The argument Church formulated has come to be known as the "slingshot."

7.1 Church's Argument

Consider this (renumbered and with brackets added) sequence from (Church, 1956, p25):[1]

(13)   Scott is [the author of Ivanhoe].

(14)   Scott is [the author of 29 Waverley novels altogether].

(15)   29 is [the number of Waverley novels Scott wrote altogether].

(16)   29 is [the number of counties in Utah].

This is a list of sentences on which the argument is based, not the argument itself. Church argues that each sentence can be seen on the basis of plausible considerations to stand for the same thing as its predecessor and the only plausible candidate for what they all stand for is the truth-value True. So sentences denote truth-values, just as Frege concluded. Circumstances will not work.

The bracketed descriptions in (13) and (14) both denote Sir Walter Scott. So, Church reasons, whatever (13) stands for, (14) must stand for

---

[1] See also (Church, 1943).

Frege's Detour: An Essay on Meaning, Reference, and Truth. John Perry, Oxford University Press (2019).
© John Perry DOI: 10.1093/oso/9780198812821.001.0001

the same thing. Call this a *substitution* step. Sentences (14) and (15) put the same demands on Scott, authorship, the number 29, and the Waverley novels as (14). So, Church reasons, this step, call it *redistribution*, must also preserve the denotation of the sentences. But then (15) leads to (16) by substitution. So, whatever sentences stands for, it seems that (13) – (16) all stand for the same one of them.

But then, Church asks, what do these sentences have in common other than their truth-value?

Church found the seeds of his slingshot in Frege. Frege does say, after having settled on truth-values as the denotations of sentences, "...in the denotation of the sentence all that is specific is obliterated." In "On Sense and Denotation" Frege's remark seems to be drawing a consequence from the conclusion that sentences denote truth-values, not providing an argument for it. Still, Church's argument does suggest how the other choices made in Frege's entire theory dictate the choice of truth-values as the denotations of sentences.

The argument turns on two principles Frege is pretty clearly committed to:

(A)   Substitution of one co-denoting term for another does not affect denotation of a sentence.

(A) justifies the substitution steps, from (13) to (14) and (15) to (16).

(B)   Sentences whose truth requires the same objects to have the same properties and stand in the same relations have the same denotation.

(B)   justifies the redistribution step, from (14) to (15).

According to Frege's theory, as we have seen, the denotation of a definite description is the object that meets the description. So it seems the substitution step should work; substitution does not change the denotations provided by the parts of the sentence, so it should not change the denotation of the whole sentence.

The redistribution step does not preserve the denotation of the parts; it does not even preserve the parts. It preserves the truth-conditions of the whole, in that ultimately the same demands are made in different ways on the same properties and objects, and so the denotation of the sentence is preserved. Perhaps the redistribution step even preserves the Thought on some interpretation of Thoughts. It will not do so on my interpretation of Thoughts as property structures. Consider:

(14)   Scott is [the author of 29 Waverley novels altogether].

(15)   29 is [the number of Waverley novels Scott wrote altogether].

On my interpretation of Frege's theory, the Thought expressed by (14) involves the senses of "Scott," "the author of 29 Waverley novels altogether," and "is." Truth requires that there are objects that fall under the first two, a concept that falls under the third, and the objects fall under the concept. With (15) the Thought expressed involves the quite different senses provided by "29" and "the number of Waverley novels Scott wrote altogether." But recall that my account basically sets some of Frege's ideas about carving up content to one side. In any case, preservation of the Thought expressed is not the issue.

It is natural to talk of the objects referred and the properties and relations predicated of them as the *subject matter* of a sentence. If I say, "Obama was born in Hawaii," I am talking about Obama and Hawaii, and predicating the relation of *having been born in*. These entities constitute the subject matter of my utterance. In the remarks quoted above Frege is telling us that in the denotation of a sentence subject-matter is obliterated. Does Church's argument draw a consequence from the obliteration of subject-matter, or provide an argument in favor of it?

Assuming Frege's treatment of definite descriptions, the identity steps in Church's argument, from (13) to (14) and from (15) to (16), do not depend on the obliteration of subject matter. There is no reason for the advocate of circumstances to reject them. In (13) and (14) the same property, being identical with Scott, is predicated of the same individual, and similarly with (15) and (16). The circumstance is the same.

But it seems that we lose track of subject matter in the redistribution step. Sentence (14) is about Scott, and predicates the property of being identical with the author of 29 Waverley novels altogether. Sentence (15) is about the number 29, and predicates the property of being the number of Waverley novels Scott wrote altogether. Sentence (14) is not about the number 29, and (15) is not about Scott. To the advocate of circumstances, the redistribution step seems like a trick. But it is not a trick without a rationale. This connects with the issue discussed in Section 2.4, where I admitted that my way conceiving of Frege's circumstances does not square with his views about "carving up content." Sentence (14) does place some demands on the number 29. It has to be the number of Waverley novels for the description to denote Scott, which it must do for the sentence to be true. And in this extended sense, (15) is about Scott. I will say that 29 and Scott are part of the *basic subject matter* of (14) and (15) respectively. In an extended sense, (14) is about the number 29. But if we want it to be a requirement on sentences having the same denotation that they have the same subject matter, we cannot appeal simply appeal to the basic subject matter. For then (13) is about the novel *Ivanhoe* and (15) is not. We might say that on Frege's theory of descriptions, all that is specific about the identifying conditions is lost in the denotation of the description. But in the step from (14) to (15) it is this lost specificity which is recovered and redistributed.

7.2 A Reflexive-Referential Analysis

We can consider truth-conditions of (13) and (14) with all the facts of denotation given. "Scott" denotes Scott, as do "the author of *Ivanhoe*" and "the author of 29 *Waverley* novels altogether, and "is" denotes identity. In this case, the two sentences identify the same circumstance, that Scott is Scott. This circumstance is what I have called the "referential truth-conditions" or "referential content."

But we can also consider the hybrid truth-conditions, where the denotations of "Scott" and "is" are given, but not the denotations of the descriptions. At this level, the sentences do not have the same truth-conditions. For (13) to be true, the description will have to denote Scott, and this requires that he wrote *Ivanhoe*. For (14) to be true, the description will have to denote Scott, and this requires that he wrote 29 *Waverley* novels altogether.

Now consider the move from (14) to (15), the redistribution move. The referential truth-conditions are quite different: Scott is Scott for (14);

29 is 29 for (15). But the hybrid truth-conditions are basically the same. Someone wrote 29 Waverly novels altogether and he is Scott, for (14). Something is the number of Waverley novels Scott wrote and it is 29 for (15).

To summarize:

	Hybrid Truth-Conditions	Referential Truth-Conditions
(13)	$\exists x(x$ wrote *Ivanhoe* & x is Scott)	Scott is Scott
(14)	$\exists x(x$ wrote 29 *Waverley* novels altogether & x is Scott)	Scott is Scott
(15)	$\exists x(x$ is the number of *Waverley* novels Scott wrote altogether & x is 29)	29 is 29
(16)	$\exists x(x$ is the number of counties in Utah & x is 29)	29 is 29

On this analysis, the we can see that the substitution and redistribution steps each preserve something of importance. Substitution preserves the referential truth-conditions, with the facts of denotation taken as given. Redistribution preserves hybrid truth-conditions, abstracting from some of the denotations of the descriptions.

But on this analysis, principles the step from (13) to (14) does not preserve the same thing as the step from (14) to (15). On the reflexive-referential analysis, the slingshot is intriguing but not convincing.

7.3 Two Conceptions of Circumstances

In Section 2.4 I distinguished between two conceptions of circumstances, which I call *circumstances as happenings* and *circumstances as states of affairs*.

Considered as happenings, it seems that facts and circumstances can be carved up in different ways, involving different objects and properties. In the *Begriffsschrift*, Frege explores different ways of carving up the same conceptual content, and so may have had the happenings conception at least partly in mind. He holds that the fact that Caesar conquered Gaul and the fact that the conquering of Gaul by Caesar occurred are the same. This suggests that facts are identical if they necessarily co-exist. The state of affairs conception does not seem adequate from this point of view. As I have said, he does not tell us much about how he thinks of circumstances.

Inspired by Bradley's debates with Russell, Olson makes an important point about the relations between the two conception of circumstances. We might think that the state of affairs that I am now typing is made factual by what is happening in my study at the present time. But it does not seem obvious that those events determine that it is *I* who is doing the typing. It seems that all these happenings could have been part of an alternative flow of happenings in which someone else —born in a different place, with different parents, but ending up by this morning just like me — was working. The most we can say is that these happenings make the state of affairs that I am typing a fact *given* that previous happenings made it the case that it is *I* who is in the room. That is, making a circumstance a fact in another incremental concept. This is an important point, which might require revision of some of the views Jon Barwise put forward in "Scenes and Other Situations" and he and I developed in *Situations and Attitudes*. But it does not present a problem for taking circumstances to be the denotations of sentences.

7.4 Quine, Føllesdal, and the Partial Recovery of Subject Matter

Along Frege's Detour, subject matter was lost, sometimes in the spirit of various interpretations of his carving up content thesis, sometimes as a result of his choice of truth-values for the denotations of sentences, and often with the help of some version of the slingshot. Some of this is documented in (Barwise and Perry, 1981).

Quine's used a version of the slingshot in his discussion of modal sentences (Quine, 1953). Quine's target is the "Aristotelian Essentialist" who claims that "Necessarily, 9 is an odd number" is true, but "Necessarily, the maximum number of Supreme Court justices is an odd number" is false.[2] Quine claimed that the principles of orthodox logic dictate that if the

---

[2] This is my example, not Quine's.

extensions of "9" and "the maximum number of Supreme Court justices" have the same extensions in the unembedded sentence, they must have the same extensions in larger sentences in which they are embedded. His argument depends on more or less the same steps on which Church relies, substitution and redistribution. The redistribution principle is that logically equivalent sentences have the same extension. The substitution step is that substituting co-extensional expressions preserves the extension of the whole.

We might suppose that the extensions vary with modal embeddings. But if the starting point is the same, the modal operator will be starting with the same extensions in both sentences, and they cannot end up with different truth values, as the Aristotelian Essentialist requires.

In his dissertation, (Føllesdal, 1961, 2004), years before Barwise and I named the slingshot and made our attempt to dismantle it in (Barwise and Perry, 1981), Dagfinn Føllesdal found a false assumption in Quine's argument. It is not part of logical orthodoxy that all singular denotation is a species of extension. Extensions are assigned by models, but there is no part of orthodox logic that requires that the denotations of all singular terms be so assigned. Variables are a case in point; a variable assignment fixes them across all the models under consideration. There is nothing in logical orthodoxy that prevents what Føllesdal calls "genuine" names, the denotation of which is fixed relative to neither models or variable assignments. If "9" is a genuine name, the variations in extension as we go from possibility to possibility, that change the extension of "the maximum number of Supreme Court justices" so it denotes an odd number is some possibilities but not in others, will have no effect on the denotation of "9." The Aristotelian can have his different truth-values for our sentences, while remaining orthodox. Føllesdal's genuine names anticipate Kripke's rigid designators, singular terms that denote or refer to the same object in any possible world. Since his dissertation was not broadly distributed, this went unnoticed for a long time. Genuine names or rigid designators allow us to keep track of subject matter in modal sentences. If we think of propositions as sets of possible worlds, we can suppose that sentences containing rigid designators provide "singular propositions" which are individuated by the individuals rigidly designated. The statement "9 is an odd number" gives us such a singular proposition, while "The maximum number of Supreme Court justices is an odd number" does not. Singular propositions basically give us abstract objects that, like lower-level circumstances, but unlike Frege's Thoughts, are individuated by objects and not just properties.

7.5 Can We Carve Up Content?

A key motivation for, and lesson from, the reflexive-referential approach is the abandonment of the doctrine of unique content. If we abandon this doctrine, we eliminate the need to find a single conception of content that satisfies all the intuitions about contents and their individuation that Frege and other philosophers have had. It seems, for example, that we will want both happenings and states of affairs in our theory. This is more or less what Barwise and I did in *Situations and Attitudes*, where situations were (more or less) happenings, but states of affairs were abstract objects constructed from properties, objects, locations and times. The relation between them was "makes factual." The situation at a space-time location, that is what happens there, makes some states of affairs factual, others non-factual, and leaves the rest undecided. It is this relation that Olson's argument suggests needs to be made incremental; a situation makes a state of affairs factual *given* other other situations when it supplies the last remaining happening needed for the state of affairs to be factual. This idea could be used to get at the concept of basic subject matter mentioned in Section 7.1. The equivalence relation among states of affairs that seemed to be needed in Section 2.5 could be *made factual by the same situations, given the same situations*.

For the purposes of trying to integrate what I take to be the core insights Frege's *Begriffsschrift* and the core insights of his theory of sense and reference, I will stick with circumstances as states of affairs, go back to calling them circumstances, and worry further about carving up content only toward the rather speculative end of this book.

8

Integrating Frege's Theories

I believe Frege could have integrated his insights from the *Begriffsschrift* and the theory of sense and denotation in to a single framework. The level of reference goes below the level of sense and above the level of denotation, which is relabelled "extension." We adopt the uniform treatment of descriptions suggested in Chapter 5.

At the time he wrote the *Begriffsschrift*, Frege thought that reference, as he conceived it there—objects, properties, and circumstances—was the natural place to start in giving an account of the truth-conditions of sentences. I agree with the author of the *Begriffsschrift*. Then we ask two additional questions that led Frege to the theory of sense and denotation: (i) How do expressions come to refer to or denote what they do? And (ii), how do we provide for the needs of extensionalist logicians, and in particular for the strategy for treating numbers as extensions of concepts, that he arrived at in *The Foundations of Arithmetic*.

The level of reference allows a simper account of predicates. The properties at the level of reference need not be individuated extensionally. The properties at the level of sense are not overburdened. "Having a kidney" and "having a heart" have the different senses, different references, but the same extension "being a conic section" and "being a second degree curve" have different senses, the same referent, and the same extension.

We may think of the three levels as reflecting different theoretical needs. The level of reference—objects, properties, and proposition including circumstances—reflects the way that ordinary people with their incomplete languages think about and deal with the world, the basic way humans organize what we perceive, remember, and learn about from others, centered on circumstances involving individuals in space and time having properties and standing in relations to one another. God may not have needed objects and circumstances to think about the possible worlds among which She would choose. But for many purposes, humans

Frege's Detour: An Essay on Meaning, Reference, and Truth. John Perry, Oxford University Press (2019).
© John Perry DOI: 10.1093/oso/9780198812821.001.0001

Table 8.1 The Integrated Theory With Uniform Treatment of Descriptions

Expression	proper name	description	predicate	sentence
	↓	↓	↓	↓
Sense	sense of the proper name	sense of the description	sense of the predicate	sense of the sentence (Thought)
	↓	↓	↓	↓
Reference	reference of proper name (object)	reference of description (property)	reference of predicate. (property)	reference of sentence (Instantiation of Thought: lower level Thought or circumstance)
	↓	↓	↓	↓
Extension	extension of proper name (object)	extension of description (course of values)	extension of predicate (course of values)	extension of sentence (truth-value)

think in terms of human possibilities, the possibilities that various objects have various properties and stand in various relations.

Thoughts are not required to be the objects of the relations of *saying that* and *believing that*, further unburdening the level of sense. Those jobs fall to circumstances. This leads to what Donald Davidson calls "semantic innocence" (Davidson, 1968). Sentences embedded in indirect discourse work just as they would if unembedded. Substitution of co-referring expressions in the embedded sentences of indirect discourse and attitude reports preserves truth.

8.1 A Flexible Theory

The framework gives us four things that words provide. They provide themselves. And they provide senses, references, and extensions.

In the case of sentences we have Thoughts, circumstances—both first level and higher level—and truth-values to work with. Each row provides conditions that, with some input from the world, determine truth-values: the extensions provided by the first three columns in the last row, and the Thoughts and circumstances provided in the rightmost column of the first two rows. The circumstances in the rightmost column of the reference line are the instantiation of the Thought in the cell above, given the references of the names, descriptions, and predicates. Here we need to use "circumstance" as including higher level circumstances, as short for "circumstance or instantiating property structure.

If we abandon the doctrine of unique content, and avail ourselves of the resources of the reflexive-referential approach we have a wide variety of truth-conditions to work with for the analysis of language.

Each cell in the scheme basically furnishes us with a question we can ask about a sentence and the expressions in it. Various combinations of answers, not necessarily drawn from the same row, can provide hybrid truth-condtioins and determine the truth-value, even in the absence of other answers, as long as we assume that they have answers.

The Integrated Theory provides a more plausible account of predicates, properties, and extensions than is available within the theory of sense and denotation by itself. The difference between "conic section" and "curve of second degree" is handled at the level of sense. The difference between "creature with a kidney" and "creature with a heart" is also involves the level of reference. In both cases, the extensions are the same. We preserve the level called "*Bedeutung*" in "On Sense and Denotation" under the name "extension," but otherwise unmolested. So objects, extensions, however we conceive of them, and truth-values can do their logical work.

In Section 4.2 I complained that if we accept the account of names in the theory of sense and reference, it seems natural that the Thought expressed by

(10)   Hesperus is moonless

would be:

   (a) That there is a unique object that is the first planet to appear in the evening sky and it is moonless.

But it seems, given the sense/denotation distinction for predicates, the Thought expressed will instead be:

   (b) That there is a unique object x and there is a unique property ϕ, such that x is the first planet to appear in the evening sky and ϕ is the property that meets condition ψ (the sense of "is moonless") and x has ϕ.

The extra existential quantifier is unintuitive, but without it we would not have an account of the cognitive significance of "Being a conic section is being a curve of second degree."

On the current scheme, we find (b) at the level of sense. It gives us a hybrid content of (10), given the senses but not the denotations. Thought (b) is the hybrid content of (10), given the senses and in addition the denotation of "is moonless." At the level of reference, we find the circumstance that Frege in the *Begriffsschrift* would have found to be the intuitive reference of (10).

The scheme allows for a natural interpretation of Donnellan's distinction between referential and attributive uses of descriptions. Consider "The murderer of Smith is insane." The Thought at the level of sense involves two quantifers: someone x is the unique murderer of Smith, some property ϕ is determined by the sense of "is insane," and x has ϕ. At the level of reference, we instantiate the second quantifier on the property of being insane, and have the Thought that the murderer of Smith is insane. This is the default reading for the sentence, and corresponds to Donnellan's attributive reading. But we also have the hybrid truth-conditions, adding as given that Jones is the murderer of Smith. Given that, the truth-conditions of the sentence are that Jones is insane, corresponding to Donnellan's referential use. On this approach, more or less that of (Korta and Perry, 2011), the referential use is a semantically grounded pragmatic phenomenon. The speaker intends to convey the circumstance or singular proposition. The semantics does not need to be changed; that proposition is available, but as a hybrid.

Donnellan holds that when a definite description is used referentially, the referent need need not fit the description. At a party I tell you, "The man with a martini is wanted on the phone," hoping you will fetch him while I am busy filling the ice bucket. You follow my gaze and see a man with a martini glass, full of clear liquid, garnished with an olive, and fetch him. But in fact he was drinking an incorrectly garnished gimlet. Donnellan says that I successfully referred to the man, in spite of the incorrect description, and said truly that he was wanted on the phone. This is intuitive, but not accounted for on the treatment just sketched; one needs to bring in a bit more machinery. I am inclined to say in this case, more or less following Brian Loar (Loar, 1976), that the information I meant to convey was that the man was wanted on the phone; apprised of the facts, I might say, "I meant that the man drinking what looks to be a martini was wanted on the phone." For a persuasive defense of Donnellan's view, see Genoveva Marti's "Direct Reference and Definite Descriptions"(Marti, 2008). Marti provides a very helpful discussion of the issues involved in "direct" or "genuine" reference in "The Essence of Genuine Reference" (Marti, 1995).

8.2 Truth in the Integrated Theory

The account of truth for sentences treated by the Integrated Theory goes as follows. The grammar and semantics of a language will determine the reflexive truth-conditions for a sentence. Given these, the reflexive truth-conditions will consist of:

(i)   the requirement that there are senses for each expression;
(ii) the requirement that each sense determines a reference;
(iii) the requirement that each reference determines a denotation;
(iv) further requirements on these senses, references and denotations determined by the grammatical structure of the sentence.

For "Booth assassinated Lincoln" we have:

$\exists S, S', S'', x, R, y, C, Th$ such that:

(i) S is the sense of "Booth," S' is the sense of "assassinated," S'' is the sense of "Lincoln;"
(ii) Th is the Thought that there are objects determined by S and S' and a relation determined by S'', and the objects stand in the relation;
(ii) The references determine by S, S' and S'' are x, R and y;
(iii) C is the instantiation of Th provided by x, R and y;
(ii) C is a fact.

Let us now take the senses as given. Let S_B, S_A, and S_L be the senses for the subexpressions, and Th be the sense for the sentence, that is, the Thought. The truth-conditions with senses given for "Booth assassinated

Lincoln," that is, what else is required for truth, given that S_B, S_A, S_L, and *Th* are the senses of the subexpressions and the sentence:

(i) $\exists x, R, y$, which are the references determined by S_B, S_A, and S_L;
(ii) C is the instantiation of *Th* provided by x, R, and y;
(iii) C is a fact.

If we now take as given that S_B determines Booth as reference, S_A determines the relation of assassinated as reference, and S_L determines Lincoln as reference, and consider what else is required for truth, we obtain the reference of the sentence, which I also call the "referential truth-conditions."

$\exists C$ such that C is the circumstance that Booth assassinated Lincoln and C is a fact.

Finally, given that $\{x|x = \text{Booth}\}$ is the denotation of "Booth," Lincoln is the denotation* of "Lincoln," and the course of values V is the denotation of "assassinated," we obtain the truth-conditions with the denotation given:

The pair consisting of Booth and Lincoln is assigned Truth by V, and hence Truth is the denotation of the sentence.

8.3 Frege and Copernicus

On the integrated theory, sentences, whether embedded or not, refer to circumstances. What a person says in asserting a sentences, and what a sincere person believes when they assert a sentence, are captured by circumstances, first level or higher-level. These circumstances do not capture the complete cognitive significance of the sentence for the person. They instantiate the Thought that has that job. We can see how this works, and why it is plausible, by considering Frege's example in "On Sense and Denotation." He begins his investigation of embedded sentences with Copernicus:

Let us compare, for instance, the two sentences "Copernicus believed that the planetary orbits are circles" and "Copernicus believed that the apparent motion of the sun is produced by the real motion of the earth." One subordinate clause can be substituted for the other without harm to the truth. The main clause and the subordinate clause together have as their sense only a single thought, and the truth of the whole includes neither the truth nor the untruth of the subordinate clause. In such cases it is not permissible to replace one expression in the subordinate clause by another having the same customary referent, but only by one having the same indirect reference.

Frege first makes the point that belief reports are not truth-functional; substituting one sentence for another does not guarantee preserving the truth of the whole report, even if the sentences have the same truth-value. Then he says that with such embedded sentences, substitution of co-denoting expressions is not permitted. It is the customary sense that must be preserved, not the customary denotation. The doctrine of indirect denotation is needed.

Let's simplify the example a bit:

(17)   Copernicus believed that the Earth moved around the sun.

On the integrated theory this tells us that Copernicus has the relation of belief to the circumstance that the Earth orbits the sun.

Suppose Copernicus expressed his belief by saying or writing, "Terra circum solem volvitur." I report:

(18)   Copernicus said that the Earth goes around the sun.

The integrated theory does not require that Copernicus used "solem" with the same sense associated with the "the sun," by the reporter, which, given that English and Latin are imperfect languages, may differ from any official meaning, provided by, say, the OED (Oxford English Dictionary) or the Society of Astronomers. All that is required is that the name that Copernicus used had a sense that determined the sun as reference, just as the one used by the reporter did. The reporter could have accurately reported what Copernicus said by pointing at the sun and saying Copernicus said the apparent motion of *that* is produced by the real motion of the Earth.

Frege would likely object that this innocent account goes wrong in not requiring the same sense be involved in Copernicus' use of "solem" and the reporter's use of "the sun." Copernicus expressed a certain Thought. The innocent theory allows the report to be true, even if the reporter's senses are not the same as Copernicus's.

But that actually seems like a good result. One virtue usually credited to Frege's account is its treatment of opacity of names. But in fact he does not give a plausible account. Who knows what sense Copernicus associated with "Solem"? Or, more to the point, do we want to count the report as untrue, if whatever that sense was, it is not the same one the reporter associated with "the sun"? Indirect discourse and the attitudes are products of imperfect languages, the speakers of which do not often worry about whether they employ the same senses as were involved in the discourse or attitudes they report.

This makes good sense on my hypothesis, that an original function that led to the development and the survival of these great inventions was their use in sharing information about objects, presented to various people in various ways. If you tell us about what you saw, or heard, or believe, or said, then, if I think you are reliable, I gain information about what I should believe. What is important is our confidence in shared reference. I need to know that the object you gained, or expressed, information about is the same one I am using the information to deal with. And, if your purpose is to share information, you will want to present it in such a way that I can be confident of this. We mainly deal with human possibilities, not Divine ones.

Our reporter may not be trying to inform anyone that the apparent motion of the sun is produced by the real movement of the Earth. Perhaps he is certain that his listeners all know that. His point may be to reflect credit on Copernicus, for realizing this so long ago. Even so, he needn't worry about which sense Copernicus associated with "solem." The example is not perfect for the point. Our reporter will likely assume, if the issue occurs to her at all, that Copernicus looked at the sun during the day, so the sun was regularly presented to him visually as it is to almost everyone, and the sense he associated with "solem" was pretty much what we associate with "the sun." A plausible hypothesis. But can we be certain that was how Copernicus was thinking of the sun when he announced at his discovery? Perhaps his main association with the word "solem" by then was the astronomical properties he had discovered it to have, not his visual impression of it. Perhaps he had worked in his study for so long he had forgotten what it was like to see the sun. Perhaps he was staring at sheets of papyrus or vellum where he had worked out the math, and the sun was represented by a symbol he invented for that purpose, and that was how he thought of the sun. Or perhaps he was severely near-sighted, capable of doing mathematics, but seeing only a blur when he looked in the direction of the sun. Unlikely, no doubt. But even if these odd circumstances obtained, it would not affect the truth of the report. The reporter and Copernicus may be like Fred and Ethel; their criterial beliefs about of the sun may differ as dramatically than Fred and Ethel's criterial beliefs about Aristotle, or more so.

If I utter (24), you most likely will not care any more about whatever sense *I* attach to my use of "the sun" than you care about whatever meaning Copernicus attached to his uses of "Sol." I'm a philosopher; hence, I may be expected to have weird views. Perhaps I think of the sun as "that posit that most people make, in the theory they develop to explain the fact that their sense-data, in certain circumstances, contain a reddish or yellow image, that takes up of parts of their inner visual space, as they look at what they call "the sky," taking up more of their inner visual space the day begins, and then less as it continues". As long as you think that the weird sense I attach picks out the sun—that is, even if we are in a rather extreme Fred and Ethel situation—you will not care.

Parallel remarks apply to (17). We know that Copernicus had a belief with the reference of the embedded sentence. We have no reason to believe that the Thought associated with the reporter's embedded sentence is the same associated with Copernicus's belief. If this were a requirement for the truth of (17), we could have no confidence that it was true. But certainly we do. Frege's account is simply not plausible.

The fact that Copernicus and the reporter believe the same circumstance does not mean that the cognitive significance of the sentence is the same for both. Attitude verbs were not designed for getting at all of the beliefs a person has that motivate his assertion of a sentence, or all the beliefs that a person will take to be true if he believes the assertion. This does not mean we cannot get at these beliefs with "believes that."

It is perfectly reasonable to say that Fred and Ethel agree that Aristotle lived for a while in Macedonia. Fred also believes that the most important thing Aristotle did, outside of his philosophy, was teaching Alexander. Ethel doubts this. That would mean that someone from Stagira wound up living in Macdeonia, whose king had laid waste to that very city. She thinks this is very surprising, and it would be even more surprising if he did favors for that king, like teaching his son.

8.4 Recapturing Our Innocence

The integrated theory provides what we need for a recognizably Frege-inspired but innocent account of indirect discourse and attitude reports. For now, we stick with Frege's propositional account, taking "says that" and "believes that" to refer to relations to propositions. But we take those propositions to be the circumstances and property structures that instantiate the Thoughts involved in the assertions and attitudes, rather than those Thoughts themselves.

Innocent accounts have the consequence that substitution of co-referring expressions will not effect the truth of the whole report. There are four potential problems, which I will call: *intensionality, the opacity of descriptions, the opacity of names and predicates*, and *logical operations on contents*. Lumping them together under "intensionality" or "opacity" is a bad idea; they are different problems with different solutions. The first three can be handled on the integrated theory. The fourth requires us to move from the propositional picture to the episode picture, and will be treated in the next chapter.

Intensionality. "Elwood believes that humans are creatures with a heart" might be true, while "Elwood believes that humans are creatures with a kidney" might be false if Elwood does not know much about anatomy. Substitution of co-extensional predicates that denote different properties may not preserve the truth of a report. This is not a problem on the integrated theory, because "creatures with a kidney" and "creatures with a heart" differ in their references so, even thought their extensions are the same, substitution may not preserve truth.

The opacity of descriptions. Substitution of definite descriptions that pick out the same object may not preserve truth. Elwood knows that the author of *Tom Sawyer* was born in Missouri, but not that the author of *Huckleberry Finn* was. This is not a problem for the integrated theory, since the descriptions refer to different properties, even though they both pick out Mark Twain.

The opacity of names and predicates. On his American Literature exam, Elwood marks "Mark Twain wrote *Huckleberry Finn*" true, but marks "Samuel Clemens wrote *Huckleberry Finn*" false. Does not this show that he believes that Mark Twain wrote *Huckleberry Finn*, but does not believe that Samuel Clemens did? There is a circle on his geometry exam with two true/false questions: "This figure a conic section" and "This figure is a curve of second degree." Elwood marks the first true, the second false. Does not this show that he believes the curve is a conic section, but not that is a curve of second degree?

8.5 The Pragmatic Strategy

It is not surprising that opacity should be a problem on the integrated theory. The insight that led to the theory of sense and denotation is that it is not just the objects we think about but how we think of them that is important. This difference is found, in the integrated theory, at the level of sense. But it is "obliterated" at the level of the reference of sentences for "Mark Twain wrote *Huckleberry Finn*" and"Samuel Clemens *Huckleberry Finn* refer to the same circumstance, as do the pair from the geometry exam.

It is important to note two uses we have for direct discourse and attitude reports. We report what a person says and believes for two separable but often entwined purposes: passing along information acquired from the agent, and providing explanations of the agent's actions. If I say "Elwood believes that his seminar starts at 3," I am supplying pretty good evidence that his seminar starts at 3. He ought to know when his own seminar starts. When we adopt the innocent view, we are implicitly taking indirect discourse and attitudes reports as having evolved primarily to serve this function. The referential contents of assertions and beliefs work fine. I identify *what* Elwood believes, and encourage you to believe the same thing.

But we also use attitude reports as explanations of behavior. Even if Elwood is wrong about the time of his seminar, and we both know it, I can explain Elwood's sudden departure from our conversation by saying that he believes his seminar starts at 3. Here what is crucial about his belief is not referential content, but its motivational power. Elwood has the sort of belief that motivates a responsible teacher who desires to be at his seminar on time, and believes that at ten minutes until 3, he must get a move on.

It is the use of such reports as explanation that accounts for our interest in how things are said and how they are believed, and our reluctance to substitute. The first interest depends on the second. If I explain Elwood's sudden departure by telling you, "Elwood told me his seminar starts at 3," you will infer that what he told me provided evidence for a certain sort of belief, the sort of belief that would motivate a responsible teacher to rush off from an interesting conversation at ten minutes until 3.

Barwise and I (1983), Nathan Salmon (1991), Scott Soames (1987), Kepa Korta and I (2011), Mark Crimmins (1992), François Recanati (1993) , Kenneth Taylor (2003), and many others have developed pragmatic accounts of our reluctance to substitute; opacity is an illusion based on taking pragmatic phenomena to be semantic phenomena. Crimmins discusses a number of them in chapter 1 of *Talk About Beliefs* (1992). Substitution of names with the same reference does not change the truth-values of attitude reports or indirect discourse reports. Our reluctance to substitute arises in cases in which the substitution can misleading; the choice of names may be important to information the report conveys in addition to its referential content.

Let's return to Hesperus and Phosphorus and our Babylonian astronomer Dan. His diary shows that he spent many years looking at the Evening Sky, and concluded that Hesperus is moonless. He spent many years looking at the Morning Sky, and concluded that Phosphorus had at least one moon. I report:

(19)   Dan said that Hesperus is moonless.

(20)   Dan said that that planet is moonless (pointing at Venus in the Evening).

(21)   Dan said that that planet is moonless (pointing at Venus in the Morning).

(22)   Dan said that Phosphorus is moonless.

(23)   Dan said that Venus is moonless.

Sentences (19) and (20) seem true and not misleading. Sentence (21) is true on the innocent account, but it seems quite misleading. The same holds for (22), only more so. Without further qualification it is definitely misleading, and it seems false. Certainly if we were discussing the Babylonians, and it was common knowledge that they did not know that Hesperus was Phosphorus, a likely response would be, "I'm sure he did not say that."

In such a conversation, however, (23) might seem fine. Using the name "Venus" somehow conveys that I'm conveying information, without suggesting which name Dan actually used. In a conversation in which the Babylonians' ignorance were not common knowledge, however, it might well suggest Dan knew more than he did, and used a name that is now involved in our unified conception of a planet that disappears last in the Morning, and appears first in the Evening.

With (22) it seem intelligible for me to add:

I do not mean to imply that Dan used the name "Phosphorus."

I might go on to explain that I cannot keep straight how the Babylonians used their two names for Venus.

With (23) I can add something like, "I do not mean to imply that he would have pointed at Venus in the Morning and said it had no moons."

That is, I can use H. P. Grice's formula for cancelling an "implicature"(Grice, 1975a). According to Grice's theory, speakers implicate claims that are not entailed by what they assert. Implications are things that go beyond the assertion that one assumes the speaker wants to convey, because that is the most natural explanation of the speaker asserting what he does, in the way he does. Most natural, that is, on the assumption that the speaker intends to be helpful.[1] When you say,

---

[1] For discussion of the use of Grice's framework in the semantics of belief, see (Crimmins, 1992), section 1.3.

"My steak needs salt" and I gather that you would like me to pass the salt, I am grasping an implicature of your utterance. You can cancel the implicature, perhaps adding, "Unfortunately, my doctor insists I avoid salt. Keep it out of my reach." Grice derives various maxims from the general principle that conversation should be helpful. Grice gives a general principle of cooperation, and derives four maxims, quality (basically, tell the truth), quantity (do not say too much or too little), relation (be relevant) and manner (avoid ambiguity and obscurity). Here we seem to have a further maxim derived from these, which Recanati call the "maxim of faithfulness" ((1993), 333):

> In reporting a belief about an object, and especially in referring to that object, use an expression which the believer himself would use (insofar as differences of language or context permit), or at least try to be faithful to the believer's own point of view, unless there are reasons for not doing so.

The cancellaltions suggested above for (22) and (23) warn the hearer that it is the referential content of of Dan's statement that I am reporting, and he shouldn't make assumptions about the words Dan actually used. That is, it seems that our reluctance to substitute can be given a pragmatic explanation, and shouldn't motivate a change in the semantics provided by innocent account.

"[I]nsofar as differences of language or context permit" and "unless there are reasons for not doing so" are important qualifications. If you tell me, "You are a fool," I cannot report this by saying "You said that you are a fool." I have to say, "You said that I am a fool." The speech I am reporting may contain a slur I will not use. It may have been sarcastic in a way irrelevant to my purpose in reporting it, which would require explanation were I to use it. And so on. If the non-feasibility is obvious, we do not need to opt out of the maxim. This is not so in the case of (21) and (22), so explicit opting out is appropriate.

As I said, I have not said anything original about opacity. My aim has been simply to show that the reflexive-referential approach can be helpful in deploying the pragmatic strategy. This is worked out in more detail in *Critical Pragmatics*.

9

Episodes and Attitudes

There is something incomplete about the innocent theory and pragmatic strategy. If saying and believing are relations to circumstances, why should it be misleading to use one name rather than another to report that the relation holds? The answer seems pretty clear. We realize that saying and believing do not simply involve agents at a time having relations to propositions. Beliefs involve mental structures with ideas as components, and these ideas are *of* various entities; assertions involve these mental states causing utterances, using words with senses and references. Cognitive states have truth-conditions, contents. But these cognitive states are episodes, in my extended use of the term. They are part of the casual realm. They have causal roles. We perform the actions we do because of our beliefs, desires and other cognitive states. We need to better understand the connection between the contents and causal roles of cognitive states to have a satisfactory semantics for attitude reports. I take some steps in this direction in this chapter.

Frege appreciated the importance of the connection between the contents and causal roles of cognitive states:

> And yet ! What value could there be for us in the eternally unchangeable which could neither undergo effects nor have effect on us? . . . How does a thought act? By being apprehended and taken to be true. This is a process in the inner world of a thinker which can have further consequences in this inner world and which, encroaching on the sphere of the will, can also make itself noticeable in the outer world. If, for example, I grasp the thought which we express by the theorem of Pythagoras, the consequence may be that I recognise it to be true and, further, that I apply it, making a decision which brings about the acceleration of masses. Thus our actions are usually prepared by thinking and judgment. And so thought can have an indirect influence on the motion

Frege's Detour: An Essay on Meaning, Reference, and Truth. John Perry, Oxford University Press (2019).
© John Perry DOI: 10.1093/oso/9780198812821.001.0001

of masses. The influence of one person on another is brought about for the most part by thoughts. One communicates a thought. How does this happen? One brings about changes in the common outside world which, perceived by another person, are supposed to induce him to apprehend a thought and take it to be true. Could the great events of world history have come about without the communication of thoughts?

But he does not tell us much more about the relations between the contents and causal roles of cognitive states and processes. The causal roles somehow have to mesh with the contents they allow us to grasp, or, as I think of it, the abstract objects that are suitable to encode their truth-conditions. I think if we dig deeper into this, we can improve our theory of attitude reports and indirect discourse. The result will be still be Fregean in the sense of being inspired by his theories, and incorporating many of his insights.

9.1 Utterances and Truth

Utterances of sentences have truth-conditions in virtue of the meanings and references of the expressions. An utterance is true if it meets its truth-conditions. Circumstances and propositions are abstract objects for keeping track of truth-conditions, but not part of those truth-conditions.

Our English-speaking Babylonian astronomer Dan says, "Hesperus is moonless." His utterance is true or false, because it has truth-conditions, which are or are not met. These conditions derive from the utterances of the name "Hesperus" and the predicate "is moonless" and the structure of the sentence they form. By uttering "Hesperus" Dan refers to Venus, for that is the planet to which that name refers in English. By uttering "is moonless" Dan refers to the property of having no moons, for that is the property the predicate refers to in English. Because of the structure of the English sentence, his utterance is true only if the object he refers to has the property he refers to. Propositions are not involved, just Dan, his utterance, and English. Because Venus has no moons, Dan's utterance is true. So what we have involved are Dan at a time, his intentional act of utterance, the words and the sentence uttered, and the meanings and references of those words. Circumstances and other sorts of propositions are not mentioned. Their relevance is merely that they capture the truth-conditions the utterance has in virtue of these other things.

Although truth does not consist of a relation to propositions on this account, it is relational. It involves relations between the utterances of expressions and the objects and properties those utterances refer to. My account is a descendant of Bertrand Russell's multiple relations theory of truth:

> We will give the name "multiple relations" to such as require more than two terms . . . Relations which have only two terms we shall call "dual relations."
>
> The theory of judgment which I am advocating is, that judgment is not a dual relation of the mind to a single objective, but a multiple relation of the mind to the various other terms with which the judgment is concerned. Thus if I judge that A loves B, that is not a relation of me to "A's love for B," but a relation between me and A and love and B. If it were a relation of me to "A's love for B", it would be impossible unless there were such a thing as "A's love for B," i.e. unless A loved B, i.e. unless the judgment were true; but in fact false judgments are possible. When the judgment is taken as a relation between me and A and love and B, the mere fact that judgment occurs does not involve any relation between its objects A and love and B. . . .((Russell, 1910), 180)[1]

Russell himself abandoned this multiple relations theory, apparently due to criticisms offered by Wittgenstein, which Russell found devastating. I think when we combine Russell's idea with the reflexive-referential approach, we get a plausible and illuminating view.

Thus when we report, "Dan said that Hesperus is moonless" we are telling a very incomplete story. We have the tools in English to tell a much more complete story. We have the apparatus of direct discourse: Dan said that Hesperus is moonless *by* saying "Hesperus is moonless." And Dan said that Phosphorus is moonless *by* saying "Hesperus is moonless." In the example from the last chapter, (22) and (23):

---

[1] Russell's theory did not win many adherents. Fredericka Moltmann is an inspiring exception (Moltmann, 2003).

(22)   Dan said that Phosphorus is moonless.

(23)   Dan said that Venus is moonless.

are misleading because of what they leave out. When we cancel the implicatures we are recognizing that the way we are reporting the assertions or attitudes can be misleading as to what actually happened when the part left unreported is not what one might naturally infer it to be. There is more to an assertion than the circumstance that captures its truth-conditions, and there is more to a belief than the circumstance that captures its truth-conditions. Direct discourse and the attitudes exemplify the incompleteness and reliance on background and context that is ubiquitous in natural language.

9.2 Truth and Attitudes

To adapt this basic picture to the attitudes it helps to be realistic about the apparatus of folk psychology: ideas are combined in various ways to constitute beliefs and other thoughts. Dan has two notions of the same planet, and has no belief in which these notions are combined with his idea of identity. We need something akin to direct discourse for cognitive states to think about this. Geach uses the section sign, "§" as a mental quotation mark (Geach, 1954), and I'll adopt this. So §Hesperus§ is the notion Dan expresses with "Hesperus," §Phosphorus§ is the notion he expresses with "Phosphorus," and §Hesperus = Phosphorus§ is a belief he does not have, that, if he had it, he would express with "Hesperus = Phosphorus."

In (Crimmins and Perry, 1989) Crimmins and I use the term "via" to articulate what is left unarticulated in ordinary reports, although we do not use Geach quotation. I will combine the two. Dan believes, via §Hesperus§ that Hesperus is moonless, and, given that Hesperus is Phosphorus and Hesperus is Venus, Dan believes via §Hesperus§ that Phosphorus is moonless and that Venus is moonless. But he believes via §Phosphorus§ that Phosphorus has a moon, Hesperus has a moon, and Venus has a moon. Confusing, but not misleading; no need for cancellation.

There is a fundamental principle of folk psychology that we need to understand. A first stab is:

> A desire and belief will motivate actions, or have a tendency to motivate actions, that will promote the satisfaction of the desires if the beliefs are true.

The fundamental principle is central to the uses we make of folk psychology. If I want you to do something, I will try to give you reason, that is, make it the case that you have desires and beliefs that are likely to motivate your doing it. I may change your beliefs. We want to go to a McDonalds, you are driving, I see a McDonald's to the right, and I tell you that there is a McDonald's there. Your old desire and your new belief motivate you to turn right. Or we both may know where the McDonald's is, but you want to wait until we find a Burger King. I tell you that if we go to McDonald's, I will pay, counting on your more or less permanent desire to save money and this new belief to create a new desire, to go to McDonald's.

The fundamental principle connects our two basic properties of cognitive states, they have *contents* and they also have *causal roles*. Perceptions affect beliefs and desires. New beliefs are not merely added to our stock; they interact with beliefs that are already there, eliminating some, increasing our confidence in others, and leading us to infer more new beliefs. And then our beliefs and desires affect our actions. This would be much too simple a sketch for a book on the philosophy of action or the philosophy of mind, but it will suffice for my purposes here.

The fundamental principle constrains the causal relations among beliefs, desires, and actions in terms of the contents of the beliefs and desires and the effects of the actions. To understand the way it works, we need to ask *which* contents are involved. If we restrict ourselves to the referential contents of the belief and desire, it makes no sense. The fact that Dan believes that Venus is moonless, and his desire to speak the truth, will not motivate him to say, "Phosphorus is moonless," or, when gazing at Venus in the morning, "That planet has no moons." Given that his belief is true, and that his $Phosphorus$ notion is of Venus, and "Phosphorus" refers to Venus, his desire would be satisfied were he to say those things. But he has no motivation to do so.

Ideas combine in various structures to form beliefs and desires; the same idea occurs in various of these cognitive episodes—which may be very enduring episodes. I use "notion" for ideas of objects. So I have a notion of Paris, which shows up in my beliefs about Paris, my memories of Paris, my desires to once again visit Paris and so on. And I have an idea of being a beautiful city, which shows up not only in my beliefs about Paris, but those about Donostia, San Francisco, and a few other cities. My belief that Paris is a beautiful city will have both reflexive and referential truth-conditions. Reflexive: There is an object my notion of Paris is *of*, a property my idea of being a beautiful city is *of*, and the object has the property. Referential: Paris is a beautiful city.

The referential contents of cognitive states almost always depend on facts that connect the notions and ideas involved with objects and properties in the external world. My notion of Paris is of Paris because it was formed years ago when I first heard about that city, and has been used to keep track of information about that city. Similarly, but more complexly, with my idea of being a beautiful city. Frege points out that expression may have a sense without having a referent. For example, "The highest prime number" has a sense, but, since there is no highest prime number, does not refer. Similarly, there can be notions and ideas that are not of anything. Intuitively, the causal roles of ideas and notions and the cognitions of which they are apart should depend on what goes on in the mind and brain, and not what goes on in the rest of the world. This is not to say that what goes on in the rest of the world does not lead to having certain ideas, notions, beliefs, and desires. But their causal relations to one another, once they are in the brain, should depend on facts about the brain.

Although not usually put in terms of reflexive and referential content, this is something we learn from Descartes and others who deal with the challenge of skepticism, from Putnam and Burge, from science fiction, and now from studies using virtual reality.

This leads to a second version of the Fundamental Principle, which relies on reflexive content:

Given relevant constraints, a desire D and a belief B will motivate a basic action M, or have a tendency of to do so, IF

   (i)   B consists of an idea and a notion or notions, and so will be true if the object(s) the notion(s) are of, instantiate the property or relation the idea is of; and

  (ii)   D consists of an idea and a notion or notions, and so will be satisfied if the object(s) the notions are of instantiate the property or relation the idea is of; and

 (iii)   IF the truth-conditions of B, as described in (i) are met, executing M will guarantee or at least significantly increase the likelihood that the conditions of satisfaction of D, as described by (ii), will be met.

9.3 Logical Manipulation Puzzles

Logical manipulation puzzles involve more than substitution of co-referential expressions.[2] They involve drawing entailments from propositions taken as the objects of and agent's belief, and assuming that if the agent is rational; she will also believe the entailments, at least if they are not too complicated. Consider once more Dan, our Babylonian astronomer. On an innocent account, (24) and (25) are true.

(24)   Dan believes that Venus is moonless.

(25)   Dan believes that Venus is has one moon.

The beliefs that make these reports true involve different modes of presentation of Venus. But the innocent account ignores this. So, on the propositional account, Dan has the belief relation to two propositions. But propositions have many necessary connections among them. The propositions at issue in (24) and (25) are incompatible. And this presents a problem. On the innocent and propositional account and assuming a

---

[2] The puzzle I discuss is sometimes called the "Richard-Soames Puzzle." See (Richard, 1983) and (Soames, S., 1985). Nathan Samon provides a very helpful discussion of the Richard-Soames puzzle in (Salmon, 1986). Soames's version led Barwise and I to rethink our treatment of the attitudes in *Situations and Attitudes*. Crimmins and I discuss Richard's version in (Crimmins and Perry, 1989). We compare our treatment there with the treatment in *Situations and Attitudes* in footnote 10.

certain amount of rationality on Dan's part, it seems we can draw the following inferences:

(26)   Dan believes that Venus is moonless and Dan believes that Venus has one moon.

so

(27)   Dan believes that Venus is moonless and that Venus has one moon.

so

(28)   Dan believes that Venus is moonless and has one moon.

so

(29)   Dan believes that there is a planet that is moonless and has one moon.

Our innocent account is committed to (26). But from the two propositions he believes, the conjunctive proposition that Venus is moonless and that Venus has one moon follows immediately, so it seems (27) should follow, given that Dan is rational. But from the conjunctive proposition it follows immediately that Venus is moonless and has one moon, so (28) should be true. And from that it immediately follows that there is a planet that is moonless and has one moon. But if (29) is true, it seems that Dan is definitely irrational. Something has gone wrong. The problem is not that (29) is misleading, but that it is false.

I think this is a serious problem for accounts, like that put forward in Chapter 8, that combine innocence with the relational view. If belief consists of a relation to a proposition, then it seems that, other thing being equal, a rational believer should believe the more or less immediate consequences of the propositions he believes. The propositions in (26)–(29) are related in ways that support the inferences. Dan is obviously bright, and I have not built anything else into the story that would block him from drawing obvious inferences.

But things look much different on the episode view. On the episode view (24) tells us that Dan has a belief, a mental episode, that involves a notion that is *of* Venus, and idea of the property of being moonless, which are components of a belief, the structure of which determines the truth-conditions of the belief, that the object the notion is of must have the property the ideas is of. Similarly for (25), except the idea involved is of the property of having one moon. Nothing in (24) and (25) requires that the same notion of Venus is involved in the two beliefs, and we know from the story it is not. But this is clearly required for the truth of (28). It requires that Dan have a notion of Venus that is part of a belief involving an idea of being moonless and having one moon, and Dan has no such belief. This is suggested by (27), required by (28), and is the basis for the move from (28) to (29). But it is not true. At the level of the reflexive contents of the beliefs reporeted, (28) and (29) do not follow from (26) and (28).

But being rational is basically a matter of being motivated to believe things that follow from the contents of one's beliefs, and not believe things the negation of which follows from the contents of one's beliefs. But which contents? Since we are dealing with motivation, a causal connection that may or may not be at work inside of Dan's brain, it has to be the the reflexive contents. So Dan is completely rational.

9.4 Today and Tomorrow

Frege raises an important topic in "The Thought":

> If someone wants to say the same today as he expressed yesterday using the word "today," he must replace this word with "yesterday." Although the thought is the same its verbal expression must be different so that the sense, which would otherwise be affected by the differing times of utterance, is readjusted. The case is the same with words like "here" and "there." In all such cases the mere wording, as it is given in writing, is not the complete expression of the thought, but the knowledge of certain accompanying conditions of utterance, which are used as means of expressing the thought, are needed for its correct apprehension. The pointing of fingers, hand movements, glances may belong here too. The same utterance containing the word "I" will express different thoughts in the mouths of different men, of which some may be true, others false. (296)

Suppose I say "Today is election day" on November 6, 2018 and "Yesterday was election day" on the next day, November 7. It seems I can get at the truth-conditions that both utterances share with "November 6, 2018 is election day," using the "is" tenselessly. Problem solved?

9.5 Kaplan's Contents and Frege's Contents

David Kaplan holds that the meanings of indexicals like "today" and "yesterday" are given by *characters*. Characters are functions from contexts to contents. Contexts are made up of agents, times, locations and worlds—I will ignore the worlds. My two utterances occur on different days, in different contexts, but take us to the same content, that we might express with "November 5, 2018 is election day." Frege anticipated this approach when he said:

> In all such cases the mere wording, as it is given in writing, is not the complete expression of the thought, but the knowledge of certain accompanying conditions of utterance, which are used as means of expressing the thought, are needed for its correct apprehension. (296)

But there is an important difference. On Kaplan's account, the content we are led to by character and context is a singular proposition, basically the circumstance consisting of a certain day, November 5, 2018, and the property of being the day of the election. Call it "Kaplan's content." But what Frege wants is a Thought, which will not have any days in it. He needs a sense for "November 5, 2018." Call that Thought "Frege's content."

We can alter the case a little to provide a "normal form" cognitive significance problem. Consider the beliefs I might express with these sentences:

(30)   Today is election day.

(31)   November 6, 2018 is election day.

(32)   Yesterday was election day.

It seems that on November 6 I might believe (30) without believing (31), or I might believe (31) without believing (30). The two have different cognitive significance. If I believe (30), I will walk to the polling place and vote, even if I do not believe (31). If I believe (31) but not (30), I will not be motivated to do this. If I tell my wife (31), and she does not vote, it seems she can reasonably complain, as we sit down after the polls have closed, "You did not tell me that *today* was election day." The next day she can say, "You did not tell me that *yesterday* was election day. Appealing to pragmatic considerations will not get me out of trouble.

Neither Kaplan's content nor Frege's content explains this. As we learned from Frege, circumstances or singular propositions simply do not capture cognitive significance. According to Kaplan's theory (30) and (31) express the same singular proposition, one I believe as I write, over a month before the election. That belief does not motivate me to go to the polls. Frege's proposition will not help either. He seems to imply that (30) and (31) express the same proposition, in which case it will not account for the difference in cognitive significance.

In ordinary imperfect languages, temporal indexicals like "today," "yesterday," "tomorrow," "now," "past", "present," and "future," and the ideas connected with them, allow us to organize our thoughts and utterances in terms of our context, the time at which the episode occurs. If we think of Kaplan's context as giving us properties of the relevant episodes, this makes sense.

On November 6, the belief I have, and would express with sentence (30), combined with my desire to be a dutiful citizen, will cause me to walk to the polling place and vote. (30) captures the success conditions of my action. Walking to the polling place is a way to vote on the day I have the belief, because if the belief is true the polling place will be open, and everything prepared for me to cast my ballot.

What is this information? What is the content of the belief that motivates me to walk to the polling place—even if I have no idea what day of the month it is?

9.6 Primitive Self-Knowledge

The first step in unraveling this problem is to adapt Kaplan's semantics to our episode based approach. A character is a function from contexts to contents. Kaplan's contexts are abstract objects, a set consisting of an agent, time, and location, if we set worlds aside. I will re-interpret them as functions from utterances and cognitive episodes to contents, with various parameters determined by the properties of the utterance or episode, including but not limited to the agent, time, and location, and call them "roles." So the role associated with "I" takes from an utterance of the expression to the speaker. When we have a thought involving what I call our "self-notion," the associated role takes us to the thinker of the thought. As Castañeda points out "I" and "now" are the *essential* indexicals. "Here" refers to the location of the agent of the utterance at the time of the utterance. Being the agent of and being the time of are the essential C-roles. But there are many derivative C-roles, such as being the flower smelled by the agent at the time, the city lived in by the agent at the time, and so forth. Let's start with something (relatively) simple.

Gertrude and Beatrice are two chickens. Actually, they are simpler versions of chickens; I should call them "proto-chickens." I am engaging in what Grice "called creature-construction" (Grice, 1975). Like ordinary chickens, their lives mostly consist of walking around the barnyard pecking at kernels of corn they see during the day, sleeping at night, and trying to steer clear of roosters. When either of them sees a kernel in front of them, she pecks. The kernel of corn plays two roles in the chicken's life in this episode; it is the object seen by the chicken at the time of perception, and the object pecked by the chicken at the time of perception plus ε. The perception causes an action and provides the information that will make it successful.

It seems that Gertrude and Beatrice can be exactly alike as far as their internal architecture goes. They have a perceptual state that carries the incremental information, given the constraints that are in force in and the normal conditions of the barnyard, that there is a kernel of corn in from of the chicken in the perceptual state. Being in this state causes the chicken to peck. The incremental information carried by the perception provides the incremental success conditions of the pecking. Given the way the world works and the normal conditions in the barnyard, this guarantees that the success conditions of the pecking are met. The pecking results in ingestion of a kernel of corn, and that nourishes the chicken.

Gertrude and Beatrice do not need self-notions or internal correlates "now." Such correlates could help them keep track of which chicken has a kernel of corn in front of her. But they do not need to do this; each chicken only picks up information *in this way* about kernels of corn in front of her.

Gertrude may learn perceptually that Beatrice has a kernel of corn in front of her. Perhaps she can even keep track of the other chickens. Perhaps if she sees timid Beatrice with a kernel of corn in front of her, she will charge and get the kernel for herself, but if she sees mean Catherine with one in front of her, she will not. It seems she needs something like notions of these chickens, and something cognitive analog of the predicate "*x* sees a kernel of corn in front of her." But there is no reason to postulate an a notion of herself, that combines with the predicate analog to yield a belief about herself. Like most animals, chickens do not seem to pass the mirror test; at any rate my proto-chickens do not.[3] The closest English sentence that would express Beatrice's state would be "Lo, a kernel," not "I see a kernel." Does Beatrice have self-knowledge? Not in the way we do. To know who one is requires being able to identify oneself by name, or in some other way that others might also use, some way that would allow identification others, or oneself, in some relevant database: the people seen, or remembered, or the list of invitees to an event. I will say that Beatrice has *primitive self-knowledge*, that is, the capacity of picking up information about herself in ways that are normally self-informative, and using that information in guiding her actions. I will include knowledge of the present moment in primitive self-knowledge.

The next example involves a more sophisticated creature. During a talk in Iraq, an Iraqi journalist threw a shoe at President George W. Bush.[4] Bush reflexively ducked. The act was reflexive, but quite rational. He knew that there was a shoe coming at him, and he did not want it to hit him in the face. Bush did not need to think, "There is a shoe coming at me now," much less "There is a shoe coming at George W. Bush on December 14, 2008 at 2 p.m." If he had had such thoughts, he might not have gotten out of the path of the shoe in time. He just reacted, rationally. Bush knew who he was, and probably knew what day it was and approximately what time it was. But this was all irrelevant. He relied on primitive self-knowledge. Chickens rely on it, presidents rely on it, and so do the rest of us. To *express* this knowledge we need "I" and "now." To understand it

---

[3] See (Gallup, 1970) and https://www.youtube.com/watch?v=8pIpPiBB4R4
[4] https://www.youtube.com/watch?v=Z61kpyZ7rIE

theoretically we need to recognize C-roles. But we do not need indexicals, or ideas or notions corresponding to them, to *have* such primitive self-knowledge.

As I said, when we say a person knows who she is, or what time it is, we require more than primitive self-knowledge. Consider an example adapted from Castañeda. George Smth is injured in a battle, acquires amnesia, loses track of time, loses his dog tags, and ends up in a hospital. He does not know who he is, and neither does anyone else. But he still knows what he might express with "*I* am the person having these thoughts and perceptions *now*." If a nurse bring him a meal, he will know which mouth he needs to put the food in, and which arms and hands he can use to do this. He uses his primitive self-knowledge. To know *who* he is, he needs some more objective way of referring to himself, associated with a notion in his mind that is involved in beliefs that go beyond immediate perception, so he has a belief he can express with something like "I am George Smith," or even "I am patient #234, the one with amnesia acquired in battle." To know *when* the meal is served he needs to be able to say what time of day it is and perhaps the date. But he does not need to know those things to enjoy the meal.

Evolutionary speaking, the need for notions of oneself or the present moment are late developments. We impelled to form new ideas and ways of cognizing the world by what Heidegger called "breakdowns," although he probably did not have chickens in mind ((Heidegger, 1962), section 16) . In human life, we depend on learning about ourselves in some of the same ways we learn about others. We need self-notions to integrate this information with our primitive self-knowledge. One can witness a breakdown, and its resolution, by looking at videos of young children put to the mirror test.[5]

9.7 Roles and Senses

Kaplan applied the apparatus of context and content only to indexicals and demonstratives, and warned against generalizing it. But I have not

---

[5] See, for example, https://www.youtube.com/watch?v=M2I0kwSua44. Of course, in speculating about Heidegger psychology I am well out of my depth.

heeded the warning. It seems that there are indefinitely many C-roles. We might think of causal theories of proper names as recognizing the C-role *the object that is the origin of the network of referring acts of which the utterance of the name is a part*, for example. It seems that whenever we think about an object which we have somehow received some information about, in a way that motivates, along with auxillary beliefs, some action or other, some C-role must be involved.

We can suppose senses to be the limiting case of roles. A sense is a constant role, taking any agent at any time and place to the same value. Our semantics for cognition looks like this:

Table 9.1 A Semantics for Belief

Cognition	Notion	Descriptive Idea	Predicative Idea	Belief
	↓	↓	↓	↓
role/sense	role/sense of the Notion	role/sense of the Descriptive Idea	role/sense of the Predicative Idea	role/sense of the Belief
	↓	↓	↓	↓
Reference	reference of the Notion (object)	reference of Descriptive Idea (property)	reference of Predicative Idea (property)	reference of Belief (instantiation of role/sense).
	↓	↓	↓	↓
Extension	extension of Notion (object)	extension of Descriptive Idea (course of values)	extension of Predicative Idea (course of values)	extension of Belief (truth-value)

With this in mind, let's return to our cognitive significance puzzle. We need to understand the content and causal roles of the beliefs expressed by:

(30)   Today is election day.

(31)   November 6, 2018 is election day.

(32)   Yesterday was election day.

The reference of an utterance of "today" is the day the utterance occurs. Having a notion corresponding to "today" requires more than the capacity for primitive self knowledge. One needs to conceptualize things in terms of 24-hour periods. But primitive knowledge is involved. I look outside and see that is sunny, in the same way that anyone could on any day. I learn that today is sunny, at least for while. If I awake believing what I could express with (30), this probably will not cause me to jump out of bed and rush to the polling place. But it should cause me to develop a plan for the day that includes doing so. At some point during the day, I should believe §Now is the time to go to the polling place§. This will not cause me to walk to the polling place quite in the way chickens are caused to peck when they see kernels of corn, or even in the way that presidents duck when reporters throw shoes at them. But if it, plus my belief §Today is election day§, plus my desire to be a good citizen, do cause me to walk to the polling place it will be rational. My truth of my beliefs will make my action successful, in promoting the satisfaction of my desire.

The belief (31) will not motivate me in this way, unless I realize that §Today is November 6, 2018 §. Apart from that, the truth of (31) does not guarantee that the conditions necessary for the success of walking to the polling place to vote. The truth of (32) guarantees that those conditions are not met, and walking to the polling place in order to vote will be quite futile.

9.8 More Possibilities

Frege's Thoughts are a realm of possibilities, the possibilities of patterns of instantiation and co-instantiation, what I have called "God's possibilities." When we grasp an empirical Thought, we grasp a possibility. When relevant events happen, they make the possibility a truth or a falsehood.

Human possibilities also include circumstances, possibilities that particular objects have various properties and stand in various relations to one another. These are usually among the possibilities we eliminate and confirm through perception and use to guide our actions. But this apparatus requires us to take a great deal of information as given, about particular objects, and also about how the world we live in works. Perception only provides with incremental information. Our ability to think in terms of circumstances ultimately depends on the more primitive parts of primitive self-knowledge.

Every organism, from worms to chickens to ordinary humans to logicians, needs to be able to harness the information that the states of its sense organs, or whatever more primitive apparatus nature has provided the organism with to eliminate and confirm possibilities. A species survives and propagates because of some such ability that proves useful for survival in a particular niche. It may not be much more reliable than chance to be useful, given a large population. It may not involve anything like ideas and thoughts. Even my proto-chickens are sophisticated compared to magnetotactic bacteria. These bacteria contain magnetosomes, iron rich particles enclosed in a membrane; the state of the magnetosome carries the information of the direction of the nearest magnetic pole, and causes the bacteria to swim in that direction, taking it deeper into the sea, away from oxygen-rich water, which is lethal. Ideas and thoughts are not needed. But but the fact that the information is about the bacterium in question, and the swimming effects that bacterium, are built in. They have (very) primitive self-knowledge, in my sense.[6]

For such cases, the relevant possibilities are not God's possibilities, nor human possibilities, circumstances involving objects and their properties, but simply the presence or absence of crucial properties of the immediate environment, the nature of the "magnetic domain" in the case of magnetotactic bacteria, that their sensors, or "ur-sensors," detect. I will call these "primitive possibilities."

I'd like to suggest that it is primitive possibilities, and the ability of creatures to confirm and eliminate them, that should replace Russell's sense-data in our epistemology. This is the basic knowledge from which all intelligence and rationality has developed, impelled by breakdowns at the level of species and eventually individuals, from the magnetotactic bacteria swimming habits, to Gertrude's pecking, to my ability to get my cup of coffee to my lips, to the logician across the hall proving a theorem. And I'd like to suggest that this is the sort of grasp of properties that we need to start with, to fully appreciate the insights of Frege's theory of senses and Thoughts. It seemed in section 4.4 he needed modes of

---

[6] When it comes to a scientific understanding of magnetotactic bacteria they are not at all "simple." What I have said is oversimple in a way appropriate for a philosopher. The *Wikipedia* article is helpful with many further references. I learned of these bacteria from Fred Dretske, who uses the term "magnetosome" for the bacteria themselves. He uses them to illustrate his theory of representation, which I have pretty much adopted. See (Dretske, 1986); see also (Israel and Perry, 1990, 1991).

presentations that did not require presenters. Primitive roles do not quite fit this description. What is presented is the value of the role for a certain agent and time. But it seems that senses for these parameters are not required for an agent at a time to grasp, in an appropriately primitive way, the property presented and react, in an appropriately primitive way to this information.

But the route from magnetotactic bacteria and their primitive grasp of properties of the magnetic domain, to a logician grasping the Thoughts needed to prove a theorem, is a long one. I have no more than the suggestion to offer. Perhaps some day I will have more to offer. Or perhaps the logician across the hall will.

9.9 Some Contrasts

The framework I am recommending is foreshadowed in my early papers, "Frege on Demonstratives" (Perry, 1977) and "The Problem of the Essential Indexical" (Perry, 1979). Both were heavily influences by the work of Hector-Neri Castañeda.[7] In the first paper I argued that to handle Castañeda's insights about indexicals and demonstratives, Frege could have incorporated roles into the category of senses, and used the roles assigned to sentences containing indexicals and demonstratives to explain their cognitive significance. Then he could have added singular propositions to the realm of Thoughts, to serve as the indirect reference of such sentences when embedded in attitude reports. I did not criticise the doctrine of indirect reference. In my terminology, one *entertained* senses and *apprehended* Thoughts. One apprehended a Thought *via* entertaining s sense. One of the examples I used was Heimson, a fellow who believed he was Hume. Heimson and Hume had something important in common, they both entertained the role/sense of "I am Hume." But there was an important difference. What Hume believed, by entertaining this sense, the Thought he apprehended, was a true singular proposition consisting

---

[7] See (Castañeda, Hector-Neri, 1999) for some of his important work on these topics. For an in-depth study of Castañeda's views and lessons we can learn from them, see Eros Corazza, *Reflecting the Mind: Indexicality and Quasi-Indexicality* (Corazza, 2004).

of himself and identity, while what Heimson believed was a false one, consisting of him, Hume, and identity.

In his paper "Attitudes de Dicto and De Se," (Lewis, 1979) David Lewis interpreted me as holding that there were two objects of belief, a singular proposition and a property. The property was basically the role, re-interpreted. He accepted the lesson I learned from Castañeda, in my terminology, the importance of roles for dealing with beliefs expressed by sentences containing indexicals and demonstratives. But he thought that what this showed was that the objects of belief are properties, not propositions. In his terminology, we *self-ascribe* properties, and called the beliefs we have "*de se*." All beliefs are *de se*.

> On the account I shall suggest, the subject's self-ascriptions are the whole of his system of beliefs. Other-ascriptions of properties are not some further beliefs along side the self-ascriptions. Beliefs are in the head; but I agree with Perry that beliefs *de re*, in general, are not. Beliefs *de re* are not really beliefs. They are states of affairs that obtain in virtue of the relations of the subject's beliefs to the *res* in question. If I am right, Perry's scheme for representing beliefs actually represents beliefs and more besides. As a scheme for representing beliefs, it is redundant. Given just a few of the first objects—those that represent the subject's self-ascriptions – and given the requisite facts not about beliefs, we have all the first and second objects of belief. (Lesis, 1979 (p.538))

He fit this view into his counterpart theory. I called the cases Castañeda and I worried about "self-locating beliefs." We were thinking about location in time and space. Lewis says:

> But not only are the subjects of attitudes spread out through time and space; also they are spread out through logical space. Some live here at our actual world, others live at other possible worlds. Admittedly, when we quantify over them we often omit all but our worldmates. But that again is a restriction we can drop at will....
>
> [We] have an enormous population spread out through space, through time, and through the worlds. That sets the stage. Now, what happens when one member of this scattered population has a propositional attitude, rightly so called? Take belief. What happens

when he believes a proposition, say the proposition that cyanoacrylate glue dissolves in acetone? Answer: he locates himself in a region of logical space. There are worlds where cyanoacrylate dissolves in acetone and worlds where it does not. He has a belief about himself: namely, that he inhabits one of the worlds where it does. Thereby he ascribes to himself the property of inhabiting one of the worlds included in the set which is the proposition that cyanoacrylate dissolves in acetone. This property that he self-ascribes is exactly the property that corresponds to the proposition that cyanoacrylate dissolves in acetone.

So it is in general. To believe a proposition is to self-ascribe the corresponding property. The property that corresponds to a proposition is a locational property: it is the property that belongs to all and only the inhabitants of a certain region of logical space. (517–518)

Lewis's theory is quite elegant, and I was very pleased to have had some influence on a philosopher from whom I had learned so much. I do not accept counterpart theory and Lewis's framework of possible worlds—I regard them as towns far along Frege's Detour. And I think he misinterpreted me a bit. But, setting those issues aside, I do not think he was right about the relative merits of our views. After his account of my view he said:

That is Perry's proposal. I am sure it works as well as mine, but it is more complicated. I doubt that the extra complexity buys anything.

But the extra complexity does buy us something. In a footnote I find rather remarkable, Lewis said:

... it seems to me unfortunate that the study of the objects of belief has become entangled with the semantic analysis of attributions of belief. I hope that in this paper I have managed to keep the topics separate. (541n).

I find this remarkable, because it seems to fly in the face of a lesson I learned from Lewis, the importance of folk-psychology in understanding our concepts of the mental (Lewis, 1966). Surely a main guide to folk-psychology is the vocabulary it provides for describing the mental, the central part of which, in the case of belief, is the way we attribute beliefs. Analysing the way we ascribe beliefs leads to appreciation of the somewhat puzzling fact I have tried to deal with in this chapter. In line with Lewis's theory of folk-psychology we expect belief-states to have causal roles. Heimson and Hume shared a state, which led them both to say things like "I am David Hume. I wrote the *A Treatise of Human Nature*." But we classify the beliefs in terms of external objects, Hume, and his Treatise. A good account needs to deal with this puzzling fact, not ignore it. Darren Bradley provides a good discussion of the relative merits of the two views in (Bradley, 2013).

In "Frege on Demonstratives" (Perry, 1977) I did not interpret myself as holding that there were two objects of belief, however. Admittedly I was not too clear. I did not reject the doctrine of indirect reference at that time. But I thought the distinction I was making between apprehending and entertaining was like the distinction between, say, where you are going and how you are getting there. I apprehend a proposition by entertaining a role, more or less as I go to Berkeley. The route I take is not a second destination, it is how I get to Berkeley. Similarly, my belief state is how I come to believe a proposition. The role is an abstract object that classifies *how* I believe what I believe, not something else I believe instead, or in addition. I think Lewis's term "self-ascription" is unfortunate, as blurring this important distinction.

I was clearer in "The Problem of the Essential Indexical" (Perry, 1979). I said there that indexicals and demonstratives posed problems for the "doctrine of propositions," which I credited to Frege. The first tenet of this doctrine was that:

.... belief is a relation between a subject and an object, the latter being denoted, in a canonical belief report, by a that-clause. So "Carter believes that Atlanta is the capital of Georgia" reports that a certain relation, believing, obtains between Carter and a certain object?at least in a suitably wide sense of the object?that Atlanta is the capital of Georgia. These objects are called propositions. (5)

The second was that such propositions do not change in truth-value, and the third that they supply what I have called here the cognitive significance of the sentences. I explained my alternative in terms of a couple of examples:

> Now consider all the good-hearted people who have ever been in a supermarket, noticed sugar on the floor, and been ready to say "I am making a mess." They all have something important in common, something that leads us to expect their next action to be that of looking into their grocery carts in search of the torn sack. Or consider all the responsible professors who have ever uttered "The department meeting is starting now." They too have something important in common; they are in a state that will lead those just down the hall to go to the meeting, those across campus to curse and feel guilty, those on leave to smile.
>
> What the members within these various groups have in common is not what they believe.
>
> We use sentences with indexicals or relativized propositions to individuate belief states, for the purposes of classifying believers in ways useful for explanation and prediction. That is, belief states individuated in this way enter into our commonsense theory about human behavior and more sophisticated theories emerging from it. We expect all good-hearted people in the state that leads them to say "I am making a mess" to examine their grocery carts, no matter what belief they have in virtue of being in that state. That we individuate belief states in this way doubtless has something to do with the fact that one criterion for being in the states we postulate—at least for articulate, sincere adults— is being disposed to utter the indexical sentence in question. A good philosophy of mind should explain this in detail; my aim is merely to get clear about what it is that needs explaining. The proposal, then, is that there is not an identity, or even an isomorphic correspondence, but only a systematic relationship between the belief states one is in and what one thereby believes. (18-19)

This view, with many additional bells and whistles, is the one I have advocated in this book. For some reason I do not begin to understand, some have thought that I was advocating something called "The *thesis* of the essential indexical," which seems to be the view that everyone needs to have a language of thought with indexicals in it (Millikan,

1990)(Cappelen and Dever, 2013). But I was dealing with the *problem* of the essential indexical: why, as Castañeda had definitively shown, can we not substitute indexicals in our explanations of what we are doing with names or descriptions of the same objects? My solution was not that indexicals are essential parts of language of thought, but that the way of indexicals work in language and the way beliefs work in causing action need to be understood in terms of roles, not propositions.[8]

---

[8] See (Perry, 1980).

10

Conclusion

Convincing or not, I have completed the jobs I set for myself. I argued Frege's arguments for indirect reference are not persuasive, even within his own theory. More importantly they are not persuasive given his insights. He could have added the levels of sense and denotation to the level of reference recognized in the *Begriffsschrift*, retaining circumstances, as the reference of sentences and truth-values as their extension, as required for his development of logicism. I argued that circumstances, considered structurally, are viable ways of classifying truth-conditions that keep track of subject-matter, which is central to understanding how imperfect languages do the jobs they evolved to do. I then sketched an account of meaning, reference, attitude reports, and truth based on the episodic view.

In the framework I recommend we can honor Frege's insights without going on Frege's Detour. By taking the circumstances (and property structures) that instantiate Thoughts as the denotations or referents of sentences, rather than truth-values, we avoid the doctrine of indirect denotation, the start of the detour.

This provides a twofold advantage. We can avoid doctrines to which the Detour leads. And, freed of the doctrines, we can provide a flexible approach to semantics and deal with the problems that seem to motivate them.

Most importantly, we abandon (A) and (B):

(A) The content of a sentence, basically its truth-conditions, can be captured by a unique proposition;

(B) This proposition is the *cognitive significance* of the sentence for semantically competent speakers and hearers.

Frege's Detour: An Essay on Meaning, Reference, and Truth. John Perry, Oxford University Press (2019).
© John Perry DOI: 10.1093/oso/9780198812821.001.0001

Looking for the single right proposition to capture the content of a sentence has been a theme of much philosophy of language. Taking them to be general propositions, inspired by Frege's Thoughts, does not fit with the way names and indexicals actually seem to work. But singular propositions or circumstances do not capture cognitive significance. Once we give up (A) and (B) we are free to employ the whole gamut of truth-conditions, reflexive, hybrid, and referential, to explain the many dimensions in involved in conveying information with language.

This leads, I claim, to acceptance of a bit of common sense. Saying things and believing things does not *consist in* standing in relations to propositions. They consist in making an utterance, or being in a mental state, that has truth-conditions, or some other sort of satisfaction conditions. Propositions are wonderful abstract objects for encoding truth-conditions, whether reflexive, hybrid, or referential. But beliefs and other attitudes do not consist in having relations to such objects.

This *episodic* view allows us to deal with another major conundrum along Frege's Detour. Are the contents of beliefs *internal*, determined by things going on inside the head? Or are contents *external*, involving objects and properties outside the head? If the former, how do we account for twin cases, and more generally, the external orientation of our descriptions of the mental, where we use ordinary words like "water" and "arthritis," "London" and "Berkeley" to describe what a person perceives, believes, or desires, and intends? If the latter, how do we account for the fact that perceptions beliefs, desires, and intentions have causal roles that to all appearances depend on what goes on inside our heads? The answer suggested here is that different contents, different levels of truth-conditions and other success conditions, are appropriate for different jobs. In particular, the logical inferences that rational people make those that emerge at the level of referential contents of their beliefs only when they are underwritten by connections of ideas captured by more reflexive levels of content.

In spite of the criticisms I have made, I regard myself as ultimately a Fregean. My metaphysics was formed studying Alfred North Whitehead's *Process and Reality* as an undergraduate. Like Whitehead, I think reality consists of things happening, what I would call events happenings or events, and he called "actual occasions." But I do not really know what happenings are. Somehow we recognize ordinary objects as uniformities across events and properties as similarities across events. But reality is not enough. We also need a realm of possibilities to understand and coordinate our thinking and speaking about objects and properties. Frege's senses and Thoughts, properties and relations of various levels structured by *falling under*, seems to me the most promising place to start. But they need to be supplemented with circumstances, to deal with the transmission of information, and roles, to fully account for cognitive significance.

My rather sketchy metaphysics leads me to think that Frege's division into three realms is a good idea. I'm pretty sure the mental realm is part of the physical realm, but it is a very special part, so for thinking about what goes on, the distinction is essential. I'd like to see some way of treating the Third Realm as a posit of the mental realm we need to make sense of things, perhaps not eternal, but evolving as language evolves and science proceeds. But I have no developed idea of how to do this. I'd like to better understand what it is to grasp a Thought, or at least to incrementally grasp a Thought; I'm hopeful that the scheme of this last chapter might lead to an account. But all I'm sure of now is that I am grasping the Thought that the right time and place for me to end this book is here and now, and I'm grasping it in a way that motivates me to do so.

List of Examples

(1) Smith believes that Berkeley is west of Santa Cruz.

(2) Smith believes that Mogidishu is the capital of Somalia.

(3) Smith says that Berkeley is west of Santa Cruz.

(4) Hesperus = Hesperus

(5) Hesperus = Phosphorus

(6) "Hesperus" and "Phosphorus" refer to the same thing.

(7) The first planet to appear in the evening sky is the last planet to disappear from the morning sky.

(8) Hesperus $\equiv$ Hesperus

(9) Hesperus $\equiv$ Phosphorus

(10) Hesperus is moonless.

(11) Phosphorus is moonless.

(12) Bratman is taller than Lawlor.

(13) Scott is [the author of Ivanhoe].

(14) Scott is [the author of 29 Waverley novels altogether].

(15) 29 is [the number of Waverley novels Scott wrote altogether].

(16) 29 is [the number of counties in Utah].

(17) Copernicus believed that the Earth goes around the sun.

(18) Copernicus said that the Earth goes around the sun.

(19) Dan said that Hesperus is moonless.

(20) Dan said that that planet is moonless (pointing at Venus in the Evening).

(21) Dan said that that planet is moonless (pointing at Venus in the Morning).

(22) Dan said that Phosphorus is moonless.

(23) Dan said that Venus is moonless.

(24) Dan believes that Venus is moonless.

(25) Dan believes that Venus is has one moon.

(26) Dan believes that Venus is moonless and Dan believes that Venus has one moon.

(27) Dan believes that Venus is moonless and that Venus has one moon.

(28) Dan believes that Venus is moonless and has one moon.

(29) Dan believes that there is a planet that is moonless and has one moon.

(30) Today is election day.

(31) November 6, 2018 is election day.

(32) Yesterday was election day.

Bibliography

(Almog et al., 1989) Almog, Joseph, John Perry and Howard Wettstein, eds., *Themes From Kaplan.* New York: Oxford University Press.

(Barwise and Perry, 1983) Barwise, Jon and John Perry. *Situations and Attitudes.* Cambridge, Mass.: Bradford-MIT, 1983. 2nd edition (Stanford, CSLI Publications, 1999).

(Barwise and Perry, 1981) Barwise, Jon and John Perry. Semantic Innocence and Uncompromising Situations. With J. Barwise. *Midwest Studies in Philosophy* 6: 387–403.

(Beaney, 1997) Beaney, Michael, Editor, 1997. *The Frege Reader.* Hoboken, Wiley-Blackwell.

(Bradley, 2013) Bradley, Darren. Dynamic Beliefs and the Passage of Time. In A. Capone & N. Feit (eds.), *Attitudes De Se: Linguistics, Epistemology, Metaphysics.* Stanford: CSLI Publications.

(Burge, 1979) Burge, Tyler. Sinning Against Frege. *The Philosophical Review,* Vol. 88, No. 3 (Jul., 1979), pp. 398–432. Reprinted in (Burge, 2005), 213–239. Page references are to the reprint.

(Burge, 1984) Burge, Tyler. Frege on The Extension of Concepts, From 1884 to 1903. *The Philosophical Review,* 93 (1984), 3–34. Reprinted in (Burge, 2005), 273–298. Page references are to the reprint.

(Burge, 2005) Burge, Tyler. *Truth, Thought, Reason: Essays on Frege.* Oxford: Oxford University Press.

(Carnap, 2004) Carnap, Rudolf. *Frege's Lectures on Logic: Carnap's Student notes, 1910–1914.* Translated and edited by Erich H Reck and Steve Awodey, based on the German text edited by Gottfried Gabrel. Chicago: Open Court.

(Cappelen and Dever, 2013) Cappelen, Herman and Josh Dever. *The Myth of the Essential Indexical* Oxford, Oxford University Press.

(Castañeda, Hector-Neri, 1999) Castañeda, Hector-Neri. *The Phenomeno-Logic of the I. Essays on Self-consciousness,* edited by James G. Hart and Tomis Kapitan. Bloomington: Indiana University Press, 1999.

(Church, 1956) Church, Alonzo. *An Introduction to Mathematical Logic.* Princeton: Princeton University Press.

(Church, 1943) Church, Alonzo. Carnap's *Introduction to Semantics. The Philosophical Review,* Vol. 52, No. 3: 298–304.

(Clapp and Lavalle, forthcoming) Clapp, Leonard and Armando Lavalle. Multi-propositionalism and Necessary A Posteriori Identity Statements.

(Corazza and Korta, 2010) Corazza, Eros and Kepa Korta. Minimalism, Contextualism, and Contentualism. In Piotr Stalmaszczyk (ed.). *Philosophy of Language and Linguistics.* Frankfurt-Heusenstamm: Onto-Verlag: 9–39.

(Corazza, 2010) Corazza, Eros. From Giorgione Sentences to Simple Sentences. *Journal of Pragmatics* 42 (2): 544–556.

(Corazza, 2004) Corazza, Eros. *Reflecting the Mind: Indexicality and Quasi-Indexicality*. Oxford: Oxford University Press.

(Corazza, 2011a) Corazza, Eros. Same-Saying, Pluri-Propositionalism, and Implicatures. *Mind & Language* 27 (5): 546–69.

(Corazza, 2011b) Corazza, Eros. Unenriched Subsentential Illocutions. *Philosophy and Phenomenological Research* 83 (3): 560–82.

(Corazza, forthcoming) Corazza, Eros, *Proper Names*.

(Corazza and Korta, 2015) Corazza, E. and K. Korta. "Frege on subject matter and identity statements." *Analysis* 75 (4): 562–565.

(Crimmins and Perry, 1989) Crimmins, Mark and John Perry. The Prince and the Phone Booth. *Journal of Philosophy* 86: 685–711. Reprinted in (Perry, 1979).

(Crimmins, 1992) Crimmins, Mark. 1992. *Talk About Beliefs*. Cambridge: MIT Press.

(Davidson, 1968) Davidson, Donald. On Saying That. *Synthese* 19 (1968–69): 130–146.

(de Ponte, Korta, and Perry, 2018) Maria del Ponte, Kepa Korta and John Perry. Truth without reference. The use of fictional names. *Topoi.* (https://link.springer.com/article/10.1007/s11245-018-9544-6).

(de Ponte, Korta, and Perry, Forthcomingb) Maria del Ponte, Kepa Korta and John Perry. Four Puzzling Paragraphs: Frege on "≡" and "= ."

(de Ponte, 2017a) de Ponte, Maria. Promises, the present, and "now." Lessons from Austin, Prior and Kamp. *Journal of Pragmatics*, 2017.

(de Ponte and Korta, 2017) de Ponte, Maria and Kepa Korta. New thoughts about old facts: On Prior's root canal. In (de Ponte and Korta, 2017): 163–178.

(de Ponte and Korta, 2017) de Ponte, Maria and Kepa Korta (eds.) *Reference and Representation in Thought and Language*. Oxford: Oxford University Press.

(Donnellan, 1966) Donnellan, Keith S. Reference and Definite Descriptions. *The Philosophical Review*, 75 (3): 281–304.

(Dummett, 1973/81) Dummett, Michael. *Frege: Philosophy of Language*. Cambridge: Harvard University Press.

(Durant, 1926) Durant, Will. *The Story of Philosophy*. New York: Simon & Schuster.

(Dretske, 1986) Dretske, Fred. Misrepresentation. In Bogdan, Radu (ed.), *Belief: Form, Content, and Function*. Oxford University Press. pp. 17–36.

(Evans, 1973) The Causal Theory of Names. *Aristotelian Society Supplementary Volume* xlvii: 187–208.

(Fine, 1982) Fine, K. First-Order Modal Theories III-Facts. *Synthese* 53: 43–22.

(Føllesdal, 1961, 2004) Føllesdal, Dagfinn. *Referential Opacity and Modal Logic*. Ph.D. thesis, Harvard University Department of Philosophy, 1961; and (with additional introductory material) New York, Routledge, 2004.

(Føllesdal, 1965) Føllesdal, Dagfinn. Quantification into causal contexts. *Boston Studies in the Philosophy of Science*. Dordrecht: Springer: 263–74.

(Føllesdal, 1968) Føllesdal, Dagfinn. Quine on modality. In Donald Davidson and Jaakko Hintikka, eds., *Words and Objections: Essays on the Work of W. V. Quine*, Dordrecht: Reidel: 175–85.

(Frege, 1879) Frege, Gottlob. *Begriffsschrift, eine der arithmetischen nachgebildete Formelsprache des reinen Denkens.* Halle.

(Frege, 1884) Gottlob Frege. *Die Grundlagen der Arithmetik. Eine logisch-mathematische Untersuchung über den Begriff der Zahl.* Breslau: Verlage Wilhelm Koebner.

(Frege, 1891a) Frege, Gottlob. Funktion und Begriff. Jena: Hermann Pohle.

(Frege, 1891b) Frege, Gottlob. Comments on Sinn and Bedeutung. Translation by Peter Long and Roger White of an unpublished work of Frege's in (Frege, 1969), 128–36; reprinted in (Beaney, 1997): 172–180.

(Frege, 1891c) Frege, Gottlob. Letter to Husserl, 24.5.1891. Translated by Hans Kaal in (Frege, 1980); reprinted in (Beaney, 1997): 149–50.

(Frege, 1892a) Frege, Gottlob, 1892. Über Sinn und Bedeutung. *Zeitschrift für Philosophische Kritik*, NF 100, 25–30.

(Frege, 1892b) Frege, Gottlob. Über Begriff und Gegenstand. *Vierteljahrsshift für wissenschaftliche Philosophie*, 16". 192–205.

(Frege, 1969) Frege, Gottlob. *Nachgelassene Schriften.* H. Hermes, F. Kambartel, and F. Kaulbach, eds. Hamburg: Felix Meiner.

(Frege, 1967) Frege, Gottlob, 1967. *Begriffsschrift, a formula language, modeled upon that of arithmetic, for pure thought.* Translation of (Frege, 1879) by Stefan Bauer-Mengelberg, in (van Heijenoort, 2002): 1–82.

(Frege, 1950) Frege, Gottlob. *The Foundations of Arithmetic. A logico-mathematical enquiry into the concept of number.* Translation of (Frege, 1884) by J. L. Austin. Oxford: Basil Blackwell.

(Frege, 1967) Frege, Gottlob. Function and Concept. Translation of (Frege, 1891a) by Peter Geach in (Beaney, 1997): 130–148.

(Frege, 1967b) Frege, Gottlob. On Concept and Object. Translation of (Frege, 1892b) by Peter Geach in (Beaney, 1997): 181–93.

(Frege, 1949) Frege, Gottlob. On Sense and Nominatum. Translation of (Frege, 1892a) by Herbert Feigl. In Herbert Feigl and Wilfrid Sellars, *Readings in Philosophical Analysis.* Appleton-Century- Crofts.

(Frege, 1960a) Frege, Gottlob, 1960a. Sense and Reference. A translation by Max Black of (Frege, 1892a). *Philosophical Review*, 57, 3: 209–30. Reprinted as "On Sense and Reference" in (Frege, 1952); page references are to the reprint. In this book, this paper is referred to as "On Sense and Denotation."

(Frege, 1893/1903) Frege, Gottlob. *Grundgesetze der Arithmetik, Band I* (1893); Band II (1903). Jena: Verlag Hermann Pohle.

(Frege, 1918a) Frege, Gottlob. *Der Gedanke. Eine logische Untersuchung. Beiträge zur Philosophie des deutschen Idealismus* I: 58–77.

(Frege, 1918b) Frege, Gottlob. *Die Verneinung. Beiträge zur Philosophie des deutschen Idealismus* I: 143–57.

(Frege, 1923) Frege, Gottlob. *Gedankenfüge. Beiträge zur Philosophie des deutschen Idealismus* I (1923): 36–51.

(Frege, 1952) Frege, Gottlob. *Translations From the Philosophical Writings of Gottlob Frege.* Edited and translated by Peter Geach and Max Black. Oxford: Basil Blackwell.

(Frege, 1977) Frege, Gottlob. *Logical Investigations*. Translations by P.T. Geach and R. H. Stoothoff of (Frege, 1918a), (Frege, 1918b), (Frege, 1923). New Haven: Yale University Press.

(Frege, 1980) Frege, Gottlob. *Philosophical and Mathematical Correspondence*. Edited by Gottfried Gabriel, Hans Hermes, Friedrich Kambartel, Christian Thiel, and Albert Veraart. Abridged from the German edition by Brian McGuiness. Translated by Hans Kaal. Chicago: The University of Chicago Press.

(French et. al., 1979) French, Peter A., Theodore E. Uehuling, Jr., and Howard K. Wettstein, eds. *Contemporary Perspectives in the Philosophy of Language*. Minneapolis: University of Minnesota Press.

(Gallup, 1970) Gallup, G.G. Jr. Chimpanzees: Self recognition. *Science*, 167: 86–87.

(Garmendia, 2015) Garmendia, Joana. A (Neo)Gricean Account of Irony: An Answer to Relevance Theory. *International Review of Pragmatics* 7: 40–79.

(Geach, 1954) Geach, Peter T. *Mental Acts*. London: Routledge & Kegan Paul.

(Genovesi, 2019) Genovesi, Chris. *Food for Thought: Metaphor in Language and Cognition*. PhD dissertation, Carleton University.

(Goldfarb, 2010) Goldfarb, Warren. *Frege's Conception of Logic*. In Michael Potter and Tom Ricketts, eds. *The Cambridge Companion to Frege*. Cambridge: Cambridge University Press.

(Grice, 1975) Grice, H.P. Method in Philosophical Psychology: From the Banal to the Bizarre. *Proceedings and Addresses of the American Philosophical Association* pp. 23–53.

(Grice, 1975a) Grice, H. P. Logic and Conversation. In P. Cole and J. Morgan (eds.), *Syntax and Semantics*, vol. 3: *Speech Acts*. Academic Press, New York, pp. 41–58.

(Hall, 1993) Hall, Lisa. *Individualism, Mental Content and Cognitive Science*. Stanford University Dissertation.

(Heidegger, 1927, 1977) Heidegger, Martin. *Sein und Zeit* in Heidegger's *Gesamtausgabe*, volume 2. F.-W. von Herrmann, editor. XIV, 586p.

(Heidegger, 1962) Heidegger, Martin. Heidegger, Martin. *Being and Time*. Translation of (Heidegger, 1927, 1977) by John Macquarrie and Edward Robinson. London: SCM Press.

(Hewitt, 2015) Hewitt Carl. *Inconsistency Robustness*. College Publications.

(Horty, 2007) Horty, John. *Frege on Definitions*. Oxford: Oxford University Press.

(Israel and Perry, 1990) Israel, David and John Perry. What is Information? In P. Hanson (ed.) *Information, Language and Cognition*. Vancouver: University of British Columbia Press.

(Israel and Perry, 1991) Israel, David and John Perry. Information and Architecture. In J. Barwise, J. M. Gawron, G. Plotkin, and S. Tutiya (eds.). *Situation Theory and Its Applications*, vol. 2. Stanford University: Center for the Study of Language and Information.

(Kaplan, 1978) Kaplan, David, 1979. Dthat. In (French et. al., 1979): 383–400.

(Kaplan, 1979) Kaplan, David, 1979. On the Logic of Demonstratives. *The Journal of Philosophical Logic*, 8: 81–98. Reprinted in (French et. al., 1979): 401–412.

(Kaplan, 1989) Kaplan, David. Demonstratives. In (Almog et al., 1989): 481–563.

(Kerry, 1885ff) Kerry, Benno. Ueber Anschauung und ihre psychische Verarbeitung in *Vierteljahrsschrift für wissenschaftliche Philosophie*, 9 (1885), 433–493; 10 (1886),

419–467; 11 (1887), 53–116, 249–307; 13 (1889), 71–124, 392–419; 14 (1890), 317–353; 15 (1891), 127–167.

(Korta and Perry, 2011) Korta, Kepa and John Perry. *Critical Pragmatics*. Cambridge: Cambridge University Press.

(Kripke, 1980) Kripke, Saul. *Naming and Necessity*. Cambridge: Harvard University Press.

(Lewis, 1966) Lewis, David. An Argument for the Identity Theory. *The Journal of Philosophy*, 63, 1: 17–25.

(Lewis, 1979) Lewis, David. Attitudes De Dicto and De Se. *The Philosophical Review*, Vol. 88, No. 4, pp. 513–543 .

(Loar, 1976) Loar, Brian. (1976) The Semantics of Singular Terms. *Philosophical Studies*. Vol. 30, No. 6: 353–377.

(Macbeth, 2005) Macbeth, Danielle. *Frege's Logic*. Cambridge, Harvard University Press.

(Marti, 1995) Marti, Genoveva, 1995. The Essence of Genuine Reference. *Journal of Philosophical Logic*, 24: 275–289.

(Marti, 2008) Marti, Genoveva. Direct reference and definite descriptions. *Dialectica*, 62, 1: 43–57.

(Millikan, 1990) Millikan, Ruth, "The Myth of the Essential Indexical," *Nous* 24.5: 723–734.

(Moltmann, 2003) Moltmann, Fredericka. Propositional Attitudes without Propositions. *Synthese* 135: 70–118.

(Olson, 1987) Olson, Kenneth. *An Essay on Facts*. Stanford: CSLI Publications.

(Perry, 1977) Perry, John, 1977. Frege on Demonstratives. *Philosophical Review*, 86, no. 4: 474–97. Reprinted in (Perry, 2000), Chapter 1.

(Perry, 1977) Perry, John. The Problem of the Essential Indexical, *Noûs* 13, no. 1: 3-21. Reprinted in (Perry, 2000), Chapter 2.

(Perry, 1980) Perry, John. Belief and Acceptance. *Midwest Studies in Philosophy* 5: 533–42. Reprinted in (Perry, 2000).

(Perry, 2000) Perry, John. *The Problem of the Essential Indexical*, Expanded edition. Stanford: CSLI.

(Perry, 1989) Perry, John. Possible Worlds and Subject Matter. In S. Allen (ed.). *Possible Worlds in Humanities, Arts and Sciences*. Berlin and New York: Walter deGruyter, 1986. Reprinted in (Perry, 2000).

(Perry, 2012a) Perry, John. 2012. *Reference and Reflexivity*, 2nd edition. Stanford: CSLI Publications.

(Perry, 2012) Perry, John, 2012. Donnellan's Blocks. In Joseph Almog and Paulo Leonardi (eds.), *The Philosophy of Keith Donnellan*. Oxford: Oxford University Press.

(Quine, 1953) Quine, W.V. Three Grades of Modal Involvement. *Proceedings of the Eleventh International Congress of Philosophy* 13:65–81.

(Quine, 1976) Quine, W.V. *Ways of Paradox*, revised and enlarged edition. Cambridge: Harvard University Press.

(Quine, 1956) Quine, W.V.O. Quantifiers and Propositional Attitudes. *The Journal of Philosophy* 53: 177–187.

(Quine, 1951) Quine, W. V. O. Two Dogmas of Empiricism. *The Philosophical Review* 60 (1): 20–43.

(Recanati, 2013) Recanati, François. *Mental Files*. Oxford: Oxford University Press.

(Recanati, 2017) Recanati, François. *Mental Files In Flux*. Oxford: Oxford University Press.

(Recanati, 1993) Recanati, François. *Direct Reference*. Oxford: Blackwells.

(Reichenbach, 1947) Reichenbach, Hans. *Elements of Symbolic Logic*.

(Richard, 1983) Richard, Mark. Direct Reference and Ascriptions of Belief, *Journal of Philosophical Logic* 12: 425–447.

(Russell, 1903) Russell, Bertrand, 1903. *The Principles of Mathematics*. Cambridge: Cambridge University Press.

(Russell, 1905) Russell, Bertrand. On Denoting. *Mind*, New Series, 14, 56: 479–493

(Russell, 1910) Russell, Bertrand. On the nature of truth and falsehood. In (Russell, 1910), 170ff.

(Russell, 1910) Russell, Bertrand. *Philosophical Essays*. London: Longmans, Green and Co.

(Runes, no date) Runes, Dagobert D. *The Dictionary Of Philosophy*. New York: Philosophical Library.

(Russell, 1919) Russell, Bertrand, 1919. *Introduction to Mathematical Philosophy*, Barnes & Noble, Inc, New York, NY.

(Salmon and Soames, 1988) Salmon, Nathan U. and Scott Soames (eds.) *Propositions and Attitudes* Oxford: Oxford University Press.

(Salmon, 1991) Salmon, Nathan. *Frege's Puzzle* Atascadero, Ca: Ridgeview Publishing.

(Salmon, 1986) Salmon, Nathan. Reflexivity. *Notre Dame Journal of Formal Logic*, vol. 27, no. 3 (July 1986), pp. 401–429; reprinted in (Salmon and Soames, 1988).

(Shoemaker, 1963) Shoemaker, Sydney. *Self-Knowledge and Self-Identity*. Ithaca: Cornell University Press.

(Shoemaker, 1968) Shoemaker, Sydney. Self-Reference and Self-Awareness. *Journal of Philosophy* (1968): 555–67.

(Sluga, 1980) Sluga, Hans. *Gottlob Frege*. London, Routledge.

(Soames, S., 1987) Soames, Scott, Direct Reference, Propositional Attitudes, and Semantic Content. *Philosophical Topics* 15, 47–87.

(Soames, S., 1985) Soames, Scott. Lost Innocence. *Linguistics and Philosophy*, Volume 8, No. 1: 59–71.

(Taylor, 2003) Taylor, Kenneth. *Reference and the Rational Mind*. Stanford: CSLI Publications.

(Vallée, 2014) Vallée, Richard, 2014. Slurring and common knowledge of ordinary language. *Journal of Pragmatics* 61 (2014) 78–90. Reprinted in (Vallée, 2018).

(Vallée, 2018) Vallée, Richard. *Words and Contents* Stanford: CSLI Publications, 2018.

(van Heijenoort, 2002) van Heijenoort, Jean. *From Frege to Godel: A Source Book in Mathematical Logic, 1879–1931.*

(Weitzman, 1989) Weitzman, Leora. *Propositional Identity and Structure in Frege*. Doctoral Dissertation, Stanford Philosophy Department.

(Wettstein, 1986) Wettstein, Howard. Has Semantics Rested on a Mistake? *The Journal of Philosophy* Vol 83, 4:185–209.

(Whitehead, 1929) Whitehead, Alfred North. (1929). *Process and Reality. An Essay in Cosmology*. New York: Macmillan.

(Zalta, 1983) Zalta, Edward N. *Abstract Objects: An Introduction to Axiomatic Metaphysics*, Dordrecht: D. Reidel, 1983.

(Zalta, 1988) Zalta, Edward N. *Intensional Logic and the Metaphysics of Intentionality*, Cambridge, MA: The MIT 1988.

Index